Chronicles

Chronicles Early Works

Dionne Brand

Foreword by
Leslie Sanders

WILFRID LAURIER
UNIVERSITY PRESS

We acknowledge the support of the Canada Council for the Arts for our publishing program. We acknowledge the financial support of the Government of Canada through the Canada Book Fund for our publishing activities.

 Canada Council for the Arts Conseil des Arts du Canada

 ONTARIO ARTS COUNCIL CONSEIL DES ARTS DE L'ONTARIO

Library and Archives Canada Cataloguing in Publication

Brand, Dionne, 1953–
    Chronicles : early works / Dionne Brand ; foreword by Leslie Sanders.

Includes three volumes previously published separately under titles: Primitive offensive, Winter epigrams & Epigrams to Ernesto Cardenal in defense of Claudia, Chronicles of the hostile sun.

ISBN 978-1-55458-374-4

    I. Title.

PS8553.R275A6 2011   C811'.54   C2011-903398-4

Cover image by Nell Painter: *Ten Warped* (digital media, 2010). Cover design by Daiva Villa, Chris Rowat Design. Text design by Catharine Bonas-Taylor.

This book is printed on FSC recycled paper and is certified Ecologo. It is made from 100% post-consumer fibre, processed chlorine free, and manufactured using biogas energy.

Printed in Canada

Published by Wilfrid Laurier University Press
Waterloo, Ontario, Canada
www.wlupress.wlu.ca

 FSC RECYCLED Paper made from recycled material FSC® C103567

Contents

Foreword

[T]he poet's duty, in truth or in error ... should be that of in a humble
way taking sides ... to join the extensive forces of the organized masses of
the people, to join with life and soul with suffering and hope, because it
is only from this great popular stream that the necessary changes can
arise for the authors and for the nations.

—*Pablo Neruda, Nobel Prize acceptance speech, 1971*

From its earliest days, Dionne Brand's creative impulse has been conceived and
nourished by the commitment of which Pablo Neruda speaks. Her work, elo-
quent and searing, explores and chronicles how history shapes human exis-
tence, in particular the lives of those ruptured and scattered by New World
slaveries and modern crises. This republication of three early volumes—*Prim-
itive Offensive, Winter Epigrams and Epigrams to Ernesto Cardenal in Defense of
Claudia*, and *Chronicles of the Hostile Sun*—returns to view the entire trajectory
of her poetic journey. Written within three years of each other, these works
together reveal the early clarity and enduring nature of her poetic intention, as
well as moments that shaped her work. Readers familiar with what came later
will find the earlier work haunting, a testament to a historical moment in which
change seemed possible, even imminent, a belief nourished by the various social
movements that galvanized a generation: African and Caribbean nations newly
liberated from the colonial yoke, various liberation struggles in Central Amer-
ica, the US civil rights and various anti-war movements, especially against the
war in Vietnam in the United States, women's rights and Stonewall, and, across
Europe, the student and worker demonstrations of 1968.

Individually and as a whole, Brand's work charts a collective as well as a
personal journey, delving into the burdens of history and the fugitive, contin-
gent, dynamic, and mutable geographies of the African diaspora. In succes-
sive volumes, the poet locates herself within matrices of language, place,

gender, sexuality, and politics. She maps what she calls the "murmurous genealogy" of her city, Toronto, and the denizen-citizenship of the contemporary global. Her work is well known for its vivid delineation of the in-between, the dynamism and stasis of "another place not here," as she titled her first novel, and for her exhaustive limning of the actualities and perils of all locations not only for Africans of the diaspora but also for the disenfranchised of the world. In her poetry, women's lives and women's bodies unselfconsciously define and constitute the human, setting in relief the partiality of male poets' constructions of idea and sentiment. Brand's work is resolutely political but not, ultimately, doctrinaire or didactic; rather, it renders palpable and vivid, "joining with life and soul, with suffering and hope," reality on the side the poet is taking.

Formally, these early works evidence Brand's exploration of what will become her signature: the long poem. Her concerns and her rhythms require its capaciousness, room in which intensity can build and amplify. All three volumes are formal experiments, principally with length and line; they also reveal influences and conversations: literary reference, attention and allusions to older poets of the Caribbean, particularly Aimé Césaire and Kamau Brathwaite, to the burgeoning Black Arts Movement in the United States, Gwendolyn Brooks, Nikki Giovanni, and to Latin American writers, particularly Pablo Neruda, Roque Dalton, and Ernesto Cardenal, and, finally, to Bertolt Brecht. The works evoke and testify to more hopeful times of international social change, when poetry was a principal expression of anti-imperialist and anti-racist resistance and of artistic efforts to develop a communal consciousness up to the task of making a new world.

These works also document a period in Toronto's history—indeed, Canada's history—marked by a significant increase in the black population, particularly as a result of a loosening of immigration requirements and an influx of students from the Caribbean. When Dionne Brand arrived in Canada in 1970 as a teenager, she and her companions came as the youth steeped in pan-African consciousness. She was well aware of freedom struggles on the African continent, throughout the diaspora, and in the Non-Aligned Movement of the so-called Third World. Inspired particularly by the civil-rights movement in the United States, Brand later wrote: "I had come to meet my compatriots at the barricades, to face the dogs and the water hoses of Bull Connors, to defy George Wallace.... When I landed in Toronto I put my luggage down in the apartment on Keele Street and headed for Harlem, the Apollo, 125th Street."[1] Although Canadians obdurately insisted that the racial battles for civil and human rights south of the border had no relevance to Canadian political and social realities, the students in Canada insisted on similarities and connections. The most famous of these took place in 1969, in Montreal's Sir George Williams (now Concordia) University, where protest over discriminatory grading practices ended with the destruction of the computer centre.

In Toronto, the black community pursued political work and a variety of social and educational initiatives to support a growing black population little understood, and not welcomed, by a city that was then predominantly anglo and socially conservative. Their work coincided with several significant movements in the US: especially the Black Arts and Black Power movements, the latter propelled by the violence of southern white resistance to the civil-rights movement as well as by the deeply entrenched racism throughout the country, and the former, an artistic movement in opposition to Western aesthetic orthodoxies, expressive of newly emerging black voices. A central tenet of the Black Arts Movement was the responsibility of artists to address social and political concerns, but the artist *engagé* is also a principle of existentialism and generally of the left political philosophy that permeated the intellectual milieu of the period's progressive politics. The artist was of necessity activist, "taking sides."

In the United States and the UK, relatively mainstream publishers promoted some of the writers who emerged in this period; for example, in the UK, Heinemann, with its African and Caribbean Writers series; in the United States, Bobbs-Merrill, Harper & Row, and Random House; and, in Canada, McClelland and Stewart, House of Anansi, and Macmillan. However, these new voices required their own outlets as well: notably, Canada in the 1970s saw the emergence of Harold Head's Khoisan Artist Books and Ann Wallace's Williams-Wallace.

Primitive Offensive (1982) is, strictly speaking, Brand's third collection of poetry. Her first effort is *'Fore day morning: poems* (1978), a collection of short lyrics, and her second is *Earth Magic* (1980), a volume for children (this was reissued with new illustrations by Kids Can Press in 2006). With *Primitive Offensive* it is already clear that a significant and distinctive voice is emerging. *Primitive Offensive* is a long poem, in fourteen cantos, with harsh yet sonorous imagery and lines that build in intensity. Epic in scope, both historical and mythical in invocation, it interjects woman's voice and women's bodies into a frequent topic of poetry of that period: the anguished and trenchant recounting of the fate of the colonized, both of the diaspora and on the continent, and, at the same time, a hopefulness about the efficacy of opposition, intellectual and social. Brand declares her intervention into the totalizing male narrative of the anti-colonial. In image, the poem recalls Aimé Césaire's *Cahier d'un retour au pays natal*; in scope of narrative Kamau Brathwaite's *The Arrivants*. Moreover, Brand shares with Pablo Neruda the use of the canto in the poetic recounting of history. Yet Brand's landscapes are her own: at times mythic, at times situated in both an African past and a present, variously Cuba, Europe, South Africa. The voice is both searching and determined. In her discussion of *Primitive Offensive*, Himani Bannerji invokes Franz Fanon of *The Wretched of the Earth*. She terms the title a war cry that both deploys and redefines "the primitive," and describes its speaker as gathering shards of the past so as to imagine a future path.[2] Readers familiar with Brand's later work, *Inventory* and *Ossuaries* in particular, will find this poem embryonic, and particularly haunting.

Brand worked on *Winter Epigrams* and *Epigrams to Ernesto Cardenal in Defense of Claudia* at the same time as *Primitive Offensive*, partly for emotional relief (personal communication). In *Epigrams* she attempts a form almost antithetical to that of *Primitive Offensive*. The epigram demands concision and wit and allows the poet to display a sustained and biting humour that she will not deploy in poetry again. Both sequences are long poems, each cohering around a central idea. In form and tone, Ernesto Cardenal's *Epigramas* are her inspiration—as is the poet himself, at that point minister of culture in the newly triumphant Sandinista government of Nicaragua and known for his eloquent and intensely political poetry. *Winter Epigrams* is a deeply ironic paean to the city Brand is coming to love. It records the loneliness of transplantation and racism's biting cold, both portrayed through the strangeness of northern seasons and weather and the way they inflect human life. Tender and funny, the epigrams form a tentative rapprochement with place. *Epigrams to Ernesto Cardenal in Defense of Claudia* reply directly to Cardenal's witty excoriation of "Claudia" for remaining largely unmoved by his devotion. The Cardenal sequence plays upon a poetic tradition of love poetry but deploys it to political ends. Portrayed as superficial and bourgeois, Claudia spurns him because of his beliefs, the poet implies. Brand's defence is equally witty. Critical of Cardenal's use and abuse of Claudia, she provides a lesson in feminist politics, despite her own confession of "love" for him.

It is this collection that drew the attention of Kamau Brathwaite, who introduces his detailed and deeply appreciative reading of the entire text by observing:

> the epigram ... closer to the nerve, to the bone, to the clear wide integrated circuits of her meaning; circuits of blood, that is, not stereo. And what else, what more a fitting form, we ask at the "end" of the reading, for exile, for loneliness, for such bleak loveliness, the winter of the IIIWorld's sense of present discontents and that quick radicle of green from which the poems spring ...[3]

Moreover, Cardenal himself acknowledged Brand in his *Memoria:*

> Nada ha quedado, sino unos epigramas que muchos han leido, especial-
> mente muchachos y muchachas. Y un librito de la poeta canadiense Dionne
> Brand, *Epigrams to Ernesto Cardenal in defense of Claudia,* en el que con un
> simpatico feminismo finge unos reproches de Claudia para mi; ficciones de
> una ficcion, porque Dios hizo que la historia que aqui he contado fuera
> una realidad ficticia.[4]

He also sent to her an anthology of his work inscribed "Para la buena amiga
Dionne Brand, que ya me escribó muy bellamente."[5]

Records of Dionne Brand's intellectual and political journey, these two
early collections emerge from a time of intense political foment, but also of
hope that struggle would be fruitful. Independence in Africa and the Caribbean,
civil rights struggles in the United States—all had experienced tragic setbacks,
but in the hearts of Brand's generation hope still endured. This hope is per-
haps clearest in the poet's interchange with Cardenal, but the conclusion of
Primitive Offensive, too, "my legs can keep going / my belly is wind" promises
no diminution of energy. In February 1983, Brand went to Grenada with CUSO
to do development work and to write. Eight months later, Maurice Bishop's
progressive government imploded and the United States invaded the island.
Brand's experiences in Grenada—of the potential of development, of the coup
that felled Bishop, and of the subsequent invasion—decimated her sense of the
possibility of revolution: *Chronicles of the Hostile Sun* provides anguished recol-
lections of those events.

Divided into three sections, "Languages," "Sieges," and "Military Occupa-
tions," *Chronicles* includes vignettes of people and scenes Brand encountered in
her work for CUSO, which required travel around the eastern Caribbean as
well as in Grenada. The first section opens with a foreshadowing: the US attack
on Nicaragua as heard and imagined in Grenada. Trauma and deep grief per-
meate the poems in this collection, primarily over the devastation of the pow-
erless by the powerful. However, also in this collection is the poignant "Amelia,"
the poet's recollection of her grandmother, who raised her. The poem is twice
reprised: "Amelia continued …" and "P.S. Amelia." The poet's grandmother is
a touchstone in this work for what endures, the recollections serving as a kind
of remembrance or reaffirmation of the ideas of justice which might cut through
the devastation. The entire collection, then, is a lament for what is lost: politi-
cally, "dream is dead / in these antilles" and also: "I am never lonely for anyone /
but you" ("P.S. Amelia"). This particular intermingling of the political and the

familial underscores the sense of loss—the deep dislocation and disorientation at this juncture in the poet's life.

The landscapes of these early volumes will reappear and echo: *Winter Epigrams* in *No Language Is Neutral*, for example, and *Chronicles of the Hostile Sun* in her·first novel, *Another Place Not Here*. In Brand's next collection, *No Language Is Neutral* (1990), she has discovered and decided her form and voice: the long line, the long poem. However, these early works withstand scrutiny and enrich our reading of what follows.

Twenty-five years later, in her tenth volume of poetry, *Ossuaries*, Brand will write: "if only I had something to tell you, from here, some good thing that would weather / the atmospheres of the last thirty years // I would put it in an envelope, / send it to my past life …" We might say that past life is here collected.

— Leslie Sanders

Notes

Thanks to Filomena Carvalho for her translations from the Spanish.

1 Brand, *A Map to the Door of No Return*, 17–18.
2 Bannerji, 51.
3 Brathwaite, 18.
4 Cardenal, 30. "Nothing has remained except for a few epigrams that many have read, especially young men and women, and a little poetry book written by the Canadian poet Dionne Brand, *Epigrams to Ernesto Cardenal in Defense of Claudia*, in which, with a charming feminism, she pretends a few reproaches from Claudia to me. Fictions of a fiction because God willed the story I have told here to be a fictitious reality."
5 "For my good friend Dionne Brand, who wrote about me so beautifully."

Works Cited

Bannerji, Himani. "Dionne Brand." In *Fifty Caribbean Writers: A Bio-bibliographical-critical Sourcebook*, Daryl Cumber Dance, ed. Westport, CT: Greenwood Publishers, 1986.

Brathwaite, Edward Kamau. "Dionne Brand's Winter Epigrams." *Canadian Literature* 105 (1985): 18–30.

Brand, Dionne. *A Map to the Door of No Return: Notes to Belonging.* Toronto: Random House Canada, 2001.

Brand, Dionne. *Ossuaries.* Toronto: McClelland & Stewart, 2010.

Cardenal, Ernesto. *Vida Perdida: Memoria I.* Fondo de Cultura Economica USA, 2003.

A Note on the Text

Corrections aside, and while respecting what I had done before, I felt that *Primitive Offensive* needed some tightening, some weeding of lines, and *Chronicles*, some punctuating control, some recess from the strong emotions that produced it, although even at this remove from the events, the last sections resisted editing.

— DB

Primitive Offensive
1983

CANTO I

Ashes head to toes
Juju belt
guinea eyes unfolded impossible
squint a sun since drenched
breasts beaded of raised skin
naked woman speaks
syllables come in dust's pace
dried, caked rim of desert mouth
naked woman speaks
run mouth, tell
when the whites come they were dead men
we did not want to touch them
we did not want to interfere in their business
after the disappearances
many times there were dead men among us
and we cursed them
and we gave them food
when the whites came they were dead men
five men died in our great battles before
guns gave us more heads of our enemies
and those who disappeared were dead men
and the dead take care of their own
for things come and they leave
enemies were dead men and whites were
    dead men
and our city and our people flourished
and died also
naked woman speak
syllables come in water's pace
long river mouth, tell.

the skulls of our enemies
were the walls of our wealth
and we filled them with food
and palm wine for our ancestors
and everywhere there were skulls
white of beaten iron and guns and
white with the ancestors' praise and
white with the breath of the whites on our land
white as of eyes on sand on humid vastness
white as the tune of fingers, brisk on dry skin
not even pursed hungry lips were as white
and the even the sorghum was as white as this
not even the dust of the goat's grounded horn
and each night became different from the next
and we stood by our fires
and left the places outside our compound
to the skulls and the disappeared and the whites
and the skulls stood on their sticks
and no one was born on the nights after
and no one joined their age mates
the disappeared stayed away and did not
help us to kill our enemies
and we ground our breasts and our teeth to
    powder
belly roped in ashes as the sky falters on the
    rainbow
naked woman speaks
syllables come in palm wine's pace
run mouth, dry.

CANTO II

ancestor dirt
ancestor snake
ancestor lice
ancestor whip
ancestor fish
ancestor slime
ancestor sea
ancestor stick
ancestor iron
ancestor bush
ancestor ship
ancestor old woman, old bead
let me feel your skin
old muscle, old stick
where are my bells?
my rattles
my condiments
my things
to fill houses and minutes,
the fete is starting
where are my things?
my mixtures
my bones
my decorations
old bread! old tamerind switch!
will you bathe me in oils,
will you tie me in white cloth?
call me by my praise name
sing me Oshun song
against this clamor,
ancestor old woman,
send my things after me
one moment old lady,
more questions,
what happened to the ocean in your leap

the boatswain, did he scan
the passage's terrible wet face
the navigator, did he blink or steer the ship
through your screaming night
the captain, did he lash two slaves to the
rigging
for example?
lady, my things
water leaden
my maps, my compass
after all, what is the political
position of stars?
drop your crusted cough
where you want,
my hands make precious things
out of phlegm
ancestor wood
ancestor dog
ancestor knife
ancestor old man
dry stick
moustache
skin and cheekbone
why didn't you remember,
why didn't you remember
the name of our ribe
why didn't you tell me
before you died
old horse
you made the white man
ride you
you shot off your leg for him
old man
the name of our tribe is all i wanted
instead you went

to the swamps and bush
and rice paddies
for the Trading Company
And they buried you in water
crocodile tears!
it would have been better
to remember the name of our tribe
now mosquitoes dance a ballet
over your grave
the old woman buried with you
wants to leave.

CANTO III

one thing for sure
dismembered woman,
when you decide
you are alone
understand,
ugly faced woman
when you decide
you are alone
when you dance
its on your own
broken face
when you eat
your own plate of stones
for blasted sure
you are alone
where do you think you're going
dismembered woman
limbs chopped off
at the ankles.
when you decide,
believe me
you are alone
sleep,
sleep,
tangential face
sleep
sleeping or waking
understand
you are alone.
diamonds
pour from your vagina
and your breasts
drip healing copper
but listen woman
dismembered continent

you are alone
see
crying fool
you want to talk in gold
you will cry in iron
you want to dig up stones
you will bury flesh
you think you don't need
oils and amulets, compelling
powder
and reliance smoke
you want to throw people
in cesspits.
understand
dismembered one
ululant
you are alone
when water falls back
land surfaces
      they're like bottle-flies
      around my anus
      look at their blue mouth on my excrement
      when my face is bandaged up
      like war,
      white and cracked
      like war
      I know
      I am alone.
      You think I don't know
      I am alone
      when my foot
      is cracked and white
      like hungry people
      I have a stick for alone
      tell them to come for me

and bring their father too
fly will light on him before day finish
my face will set up
like the sky for rain
for them
tell them to come for me
and bring their brother too
all that can happen to me
has happened
I have a big stick for alone.
I was sent
to this cave
I went out one day like a fool
to this cave
to find clay
to dig up metals
to decorate my bare and painful breasts
water and clay
for a poultice
for this gash
to find a map, an imprint
anywhere
would have kept me calm,
anywhere
with description.
instead
I found
a piece of this,
a tooth,
a bit of food
hung on,
a metatarsal
which resembled mine,
something else
like a note, musical

ting ting!
but of so little pitch
so little lasting
perhaps it was my voice
and this too
a suggestion
an insinuation
so slight
it may be untrue
something moving
over the brow
as with eyes closed to black
the sensate pole
the middle of a dance
no, I cannot say dance
it exaggerates;
a bit of image
a motion close to sound
a sound imaged on my retina
resembling sound.
a sound seen out of the corner of my eye
a motion heard on my inner ear
I pored over these
like a palaeontologist
I dusted them
like an
archaeologist
a swatch of cloth, skin
artless
coarse utility
but not enough.
yes enough
still only a bit
of paint, of dye
on a stone

I cannot say crude
but a crude thing
nevertheless
a hair
a marking
that of a fingernail to rock
wounded scratch
I handled these like
a papyrologist
contours
a desert sprung here
migrations
a table land
jutting up,
artful
covert, mud
I noted these
like a geopolitical
scientist
I will
take
any evidence of me
even that carved
in the sky
by the fingerprints of clouds
everyday
even those
that do not hold
a wind's impression.

CANTO IV

dry water
brackish dust
base days hurrying base days
primordial journey
blistered, chafed,
let me through
let me up
whose is this in my hand
whose green purple entrails
veined, prurigenous, fetid
mine?
tote it?
through this place?
wet land
rotted wood
this humus body
plant and blood
excreta
dead things weigh me down
this obsidian plain
bald
dead things
dead leaves
dead hair
dead nails
tongue, a swollen flower
glottis, choked with roots
my teeth fall bloodless
a damp mange covers me
I cough a velvet petalled herb
my neck bleeds
ants sprout hills on my head
leave wings in my blood
red feast of my blood
fat leaves of my blood

pressed against me,
dead mud,
i have never lived,
this thing changes me
so often
obscene
dead clatter
sepulchral smell of my limbs
the sun embedded
in my skull
dung heap of my bones
my eyes are dead
they want to talk stone,
the lagoon is burning
green day of my death
there is nothing
that I remember
days collapse
fall on each other
hours collapse
days remain new
obscure primeval
hot faced labyrinths
stone and water
molten water
cannot clean my eyes
dead things
dead years contrive
secret dead windows
ah jewel of air
sepulture of air
my veined face
gestates
mornings before
the day of my death,

each side of me
the dust smoke smell days
i am lost again
wild for a wet rock,
blowing air through a stick
wild to grunt
wild to whistle
squeezing my feet
into my belly
wild to plummet,
spectral note
spectral buzz
spectral spider
laying eggs,
gnawing through my skull
lying there, picked clean
among other bones
in this eyrie
this place of clawed feet
I am bird's treasure
my ear against its wings,
imponderable
slate wings
fasten me to one day,
at every step
something falls,
legs about to leave me,
ephemeral dross
where am I
that I am transparent, blue winged
yet cannot move
where insect eyed in corners of dead sunlight,
light coffined in dust
long travelled shafts,
where am I

beetle legged, dust-crisp in rigor,
my arms are sand
twigs make my vertebrae
twigs and faeces
dust ensanguined
now I bleed water
soon I will bleed dirt;
my eyes
are pus bags
pus of anger
ground teeth
bitten bone
dry spittle
pus of my insides
sand of my insides
I cannot see
barren flower
lance of laughter
ghosts of things
scraps of propositions
bargains of mud;
hot stink breath
of the sun
my belly is wind
harsh
shine
corbeau's meat,
hegemon
of sticks
wet
acrid
bag ribs of rain
drought
jealous sweat;
of husks

pigs's mud
fibre, chicken feathers.
hegemon
of huts
bound with salt,
twine,
my belly is rope
bread of wood
chalk
teeth of chalk,
a stellate of chalk wings
on its distended point
i know that stone,
i've dance on it
often enough,
friend stone
friend foot
dead stone
i know that dance,
i've …
i know that stone,
dead stone
in my throat
that stone of spit
i've danced on it
often enough.
i eat myself
dance my smudgy dance
powder step
chalk move
paper leap.
hegemon
of adjectives,
kites, absences
feathers

guesses
chances, string
hats, tambourines
costumes, disguises
bells
dry seeds, powder
of dry leaves
glass pieces
paints
mules
octaves
rum, clarinet
arrow, oils,
hegemon
of receptacles
conveniences
baffling flags
gaping anthems.
rumour
of a day,
I move very lightly
in you,
day of tin rain
metal teeth
electric
configurations,
day
embroidered with cuts
flesh eating metals
sore glitter
ornaments of grief,
day of wire spit
you rise from my back,
this bed of ash,
as if

you want to kill me
press me into jade
grind me into blue stone
for a broken pot
if I could fall
charred breath
on my lips
dead bird of my lungs
flour bag wings
of my lungs
be sirens
yellow
and piercing
disturb
this place
gulp
glitter
break
take over
or be hard,
the present is empty
winds must have scratched it away since then.
I am too much weight for myself
too much breath
too much mourn
too little air in my chest
slave of my limbs
my mother's gestures
I precede myself
in bones
in hollows, basins
flesh of novena candles
juju
cemeteries in tree spines
Gods in big toes

bath of chicken blood
houngan, sing Oshun song for me
I need to talk to her, the only one I remember
give me a tongue
I've ...
ta tat a, dip, de de bop
I know that stone
hands
growing worse
these votive cows
this gruel
this white ashes
to sprinkle me
with seriousness,
this dance
to tell lies to my legs
rigored twitch of my legs
this is no dance
rip de de bop
I've danced ...
I know ...
all that is left me
pulled back
to the shrubs
leafless baobab
murdering sun
red in my eyes,
waterless from seeing
seeing each night, each place
unrecognizable
red in my eyes
they cannot close
I don't have the belly for that
broken pot of a sun,
which place
am I trying to remember
like a tune,

legato of ashes, nothing, iron
broad, dense ear
air of thick stone
wife to rock
daughter to fish
eye to stunned beach,
caves to hold my freeness
Spanish galleons lying off,
doubloons to fill caves,
two looks
one before, one behind
still
still dead air
battler of wind
of wind and rope
escaped feather
still
dead air,
there is a thing
I want to be
there is an endness
to it
a dreadful metal
to it
a greyness in its look
a writhing crack in its mouth,
shroud
my face is stone
shroud
my face is stone
broken into
cut and stained.
face of air
face of torn rag
workcloth of my face,
stone.

CANTO V

still
I can eat flour
I can eat salt
I can eat stone
and oil
I can eat barbed wire
I can eat whatever is left
I can grow fat
on split atoms
I can eat toenails
I can eat their toenails
and their flesh
and my own flesh also
I can eat galvanized zinc
and cockroaches
my mouth waters
for radioactive morsels
I can run like hell
to the bushes of
some continent
to Orinoco maybe or the Okigwe plateau
some room strangled by lianas
and tree lice
walled with indefinite
pungent weeds
some wasted stretch, eaten by snakes and bush
that no vulturine mouth
can pronounce
I am not frightened
I am dead already
I can run without
my sarcophagus
without my earth hole
without my bones, my grandmother's sheet
they know me,
they will follow,

I am a liar, I procrastinate,
my teeth
don't want to die
they want to chatter
something soft and bland
they want to chew hot peppers
my limbs don't want to die
don't want to feel the
slightest pain
they like to act
to bend and flex themselves
they like to take their lead
from the sky
they want to jump and bounce
they want to play that little
game with gravity
so I'll run
and maybe one thursday
in some year
perhaps 3050 p.n. (post nuclear)
if I remember and if
I stand just so
in some longitudinal
passage of light
and if it strikes me
and if the shadow I cast
sees a nude eye
before or after noon
and if the sun is on the ground
and if the ground is in the sky
and if a tree grows from my breasts
i'll come out
and then having become rough and short
and green, and brittle-legged
some solar-winged brutal contraption,
will surprise me

CANTO VI

you, in the square,
you in the square of Koln
in the square before that huge destructive
cathedral
what are you doing there
playing a drum
you, who pretend not to recognize me
you worshipper of insolubles
I know you slipped, ripped on your tie
the one given to you at the bazaar where
they auctioned off your beard
you lay in white sheets for some years
then fled
to the square
grabbing these colors, red, green, gold like
some bright tings
to tie your head and bind you to some place
grabbing this flute
this drum
this needle and syringe
this far from Lagos,
and you, the other day in Vlissengen,
I was so shocked to see you
in your bathing suit
on that white beach in Holland
what were you doing there
and again the other night
I saw you in Paris near St. Michel Metro
dressed like that
dressed as if you were lost,
Madagascar woman, hand full of pomme frites
rushing to your mouth
looking at me
as if you did not know me
I was hurt

so hurt on Pont Neuf
so hurt to see us
so lost
maybe rushing
off to some
dog work in Porte de Vincennes
or maybe to press hair
in that shop in Strasbourg-Saint-Denis
that shop, already out of place
the latest white sex symbol was in the window,
in corn rows,
and me too
here in this mortuary
of ice,
my face
like a dull pick,
I wondered if
If I resembled you,
did you get my dead salutation
I sent it
dropped it as a dried
rose at your feet,
me too
on all fours
in this decayed wood
waiting

but I stayed clear
of Bordeaux and Nantes,
no more trading me
for wine and dried turtles,
oh yes
I could feel their breath
on my neck,
the lords of trade and plantations
not me
not Bordeaux
not Marseilles
not for sugar
not for indigo
not for cotton.
I went to Paris
to where shortarsed Napoleon said,
'get that nigger Toussaint,'
Toussaint, who was too gentle,
He should have met Dassalines,
I went there to start a war
for the wars we never started
to burn the Code Noir
on the Champs Elysees.
So hurt in Paris
Senegal man
trying to sell them
trinkets
miniatures of Africa
goat tail fly swatters
hand drums
flutes, toumpans
you didn't see me,
there was a hum between us
refractory
light about us,
you sold a few things along the Seine that night,

I hoped you read Fanon
and this was just a scam
but I knew it was your life
because your dry face
was my dry face
your eyes were
too quick
too easy to become lovers
too urgent
it would be minutes
before they would be in our room
in our bed
touching our skin
like silk for sale
palms
wanting more
wooden
rhinoceroses
ivory
fertility gods
monkey tail
flyswatters
filling up our room
wanting
lion skins for mats
pricing our genitals
for tassels, victory regalia,
don't look at me, man
we need the business.

I saw what you did
gendarmes
what you did to the
old man on the train
you took him to the middle of the car
and searched him and squeezed him

and laughed
because he was afraid,
he could have been my grandfather
he tried to explain,
his passport
was in his luggage
the man with the other uniform
in Gare du Nord
but, I don't understand
but I am a ...
the man with whistle
but I am a ...
but I have money ....
what ... you're touching me
look at my face
I am a ...
corpse
I have met another corpse,
he was going to his son
in Heidelberg
his son
had a scholarship
his son was studying
german linguistics for negritude
in Senegal
he tried to explain,
he could have been my grandfather
but you jabbed his ribs,
he did not want to stay in your country
he said he had a shop
in Dakar, reflection, rhinestone
of France.
he was astonished
I will not forget you, gendarmes.

CANTO VII

guajiro making flip-flops on the wing tip of
the American airline
they decided,
hot,
canival along the Malecon,
cerveza,
Jose, Miguel, Carlos,
I met them twenty years later,
Luis though, still dances for the turistas,
Havana twinkles
defiant, frightening,
all the lights are on,
this decision they made
so clear, so bright,
with everything so much bigger.
the wing of the plane dips,
aren't they afraid?
it could be a bomber,
and they in the street!
Jorge Roberto Flores is sixteen,
he speaks English and Russian,
Jorge Roberto Flores said,
that is the museum of the revolution,
there are many things in there
this thing I can't put my finger on
only now and then a quick look,
Granma
and every chicken truck turned
tank and armed convoy,
guajiro turning cartwheels on the wing tip of
my airplane
threatening Havana with its powerful steel
influence,
a woman, she, black
and old said,

somos familia,
I could not understand,
it was Spanish
so she touched my skin
todos, todos familia eh!
Yes, Si! I said
to be recognised
she knew me
and two others did too,
one night in the Amphiteatro de La Avenida de
    Las Puertas
and then in Parc Maceo
recognized me
guajiro doing handstands on the nose of the
    airliner
with its uncertain purpose,
my friend thinks
socialists don't get drunk,
cerveza! treinte cinco centavos
carnival along the Malecon
companeros, companeras
so certain
defiant, frightening,
all the lights in Havana are on.

1513, Havana

and when it was
Encomendero in Cuba
De Las Casas, the viceregent
drained
a continent of blood
to write the Common Book of Prayer
even as he walks
his quill drips
even his quill
is made of my tail feather
feather of balance
feather of gold
but this little pale viceregent
in his little pale robe
hail marys embroider his blue lips,
still he is not alone,
his acolytes bear his accoutrements
lingeringly, kindly, even now
his sperm atonement on his dry hands,
lizards eat on the latrine floor,
that left, soaks into the oppressed
ground
and brings up dead
bodies from the bush,
terrors legate
scribes a hecatomb of this Antillian
archiplago
scribes desert, Bantustans to a continent
still plundered,
condemned to these Antilles
fallen into the hell of them
De Las Casas
ecclesiastic nostrils
scent for gold
scent for sweat

scent delicate
keen
ecclesiastic nose hairs,
blood kisses
the cord around his vestments
the hem of his communion skirt
the edges of his communion slippers
the Romanesque set of the stone in this
communion ring
the light ric-rac braid of his
communion sash
the fawning glint of his communion chain
the host he consecrates in the eucharist
clot in his Eucharistic wine cup,
hostia
hostage in the vestry,
fingers of a counting house clerk
he counts me on this chaplet
for Ferdinand and Isabella
for Napoleon the little emperor
for virgin mother, child, and canon,
the cataclysmic murmur of his breath,
"we adore you oh Christ
and we bless you because
by your holy cross you have
redeemed the world"

Toussaint, I loved you
as soon as I saw you
on that weevil eaten page
in 1961,
I learned to read for you
from that book with
no preface and no owner
you waited for me

hundreds of years,
I learned to read for you
from that book with
no preface and no owner,
about how
a French courtesan
in Cap Haitien
threw
a black woman,
the cook,
into the hot oven because
the hens were not baked
to her liking;
about how
Dessalines was terrible
in war;
Toussaint, I loved you
as soon as I saw you
on that mice shit page
in '61.
Dessalines you were right
I can hear that cry of yours
ripping through that night,
night of privateers
night of fat planters
leave nothing
leave nothing white behind you
Toussaint heard too late
when it was cold in Joux.

CANTO VIII

a belly, elongated, balloons somewhere,
a hideous thing comes for me,
if I close the window
I'll stifle on the ratty air,
Stay! Leave off my throat
no calmness now, I'll rage
my hair will curl its tight ringlets
around your neck,
my teeth will wait for your flesh,
my breath
will scorch your bones to dust
leaving its stench in your wask,
I'll spew you into the sea
like the pit of a lime,
then be a scavenger bird craning
on a rock
to pounce on what is left,
Even then,
I will not leave you alone,
I'll scour the sand and stones
for your heart, strip it
with my gnarled toe nails,
till for the seaweed you are gone,
depending from which continent I spring
Europe, Africa,
It will be honour or savagery.

CANTO IX

What a morning, Rockeffer
What a morning!
when you and I
are the same
finally, dead
a morning when you ended
as I continue
but not really
you died, your stomach
lined with caviar
mine with barbed wire
what a funeral, Rockefeller
what a funeral!
you, dressed in your casket
me carrying mine
for days, I have counted
sometimes sparingly
deliberately miscounting
to avoid living them,
Now we can talk
dressed in the same uniform –
never mind you have attendants –
I count one year as one day, Rockefeller
it works out so that I have
less to go through
you count each day separately, don't you?
Savouring them I suppose,
I bet you even count nights
not me
nights are too dangerous
my hands get itchy
for Molotov cocktails
for rocks and knives
The noise of you sleeping quietly
keeps me awake,

I saw where they buried you Rockefeller
At night, I prance over your grave
like a stormtrooper
in my hobnailed boots
I prance until my legs are exhausted
but you know me Rockefeller
every morning I smooth your grave over again
I am your gravekeeper
I put fresh flowers
I stick them where I think your teeth are,
I prepare for another dance party
when I crush them
what a morning Rockefeller
what a morning!
You bought it
you bought what I get for free.

CANTO X

Then I find myself
rushing about, inadequately
knowing something
and part of something
never everything
or enough
and not yet
and only when I
remember
Then
I find myself
standing still
half deaf
or only hearing
half the thing
and each time
it is not the same half
but it is never the whole
then I find myself
not found
longer than ever
not yet
and then
shortly
I am dead
and you would think that it ended there
you would hope
you would think
it was enough,
instead,
I find my corpse
determined
ambivalent
contradictory.

come away
                    this house is never quite right
                    it always looks uncertain
                    the walls
                    their eyebrows are raised
                    the room looks as if the rent
                    has not been paid
                    it is sure I cannot stay
                    this house looks skeptical
                    this room is so nervous
                    I'm clearing off
                    it scared me
                    I don't like houses
                    they're so ... safe
                    I don't like how they stand
                    as if nothing is going to happen

Finally, what I have suspected
all along is true
I am exactly who I thought
I was, dreamed I was,
mockingly
exactly what I seemed to be,
scarce, bare,
this time I should have
made no excuses,
this time I should have come home
and hung myself.

CANTO XI

we die badly
always
public and graceless
sixteen of us
bloods mixed in on a bus
bombed
without names,
in our mirrors, in our hands, in newspapers,
in stained rooms,
wrestling with piss and shit
in gutters
for room to die
on Cape town pavements
in contorted embrace with stone
stone the perverse
lascivious for flying lovers
we fall out of windows
as if we do not know how to use
doors
or perhaps there are no doors Jo'burg
only windows
laid down as traps for us to fall
out of windows only ten feet below
we are not cats
we fall one hundred feet
particles of our hair and skin
on wooden clubs
and concrete banisters
in our houses
on Sunday mornings
in Toronto
if the police say we're wielding
machetes
on Atlantic river banks
black thread tangled up

embroidering sinister
and on the radio
in phrases
about innocent missionaries
and so many hundreds of us without lineage
without mothers to call us by name.

CANTO XII

goodnight from Pretoria
goodnight from Pretoria
the Professor answered the radio announcer
the Professor was skeptical about ...
the national party would not be pressured
the national party was skeptical about humanity
the radio announcer would not be pressured
goodnight from Pretoria.
About four o'clock in the morning
when the door gets cold
and the glass wants to cake and crumble
as the bigness
presses against the house,
fills up the spaces
where it has pushed us back,
and the street shivers,
pees itself,
and something, some spot, some absence,
some resonance of it,
stings a stray mangy dog
into a yelp,
strings his tail in the air,
flings his jaw useless,
his nails dig into the asphalt
hopelessly,
running ...
what difference?
the dog and me
in excruciating arabesque.

There between the bush
ingratiating....
between the leaves
hanging cold opaque cloth
slender ...

my exquisite improvisation
broken
a feeling of bowels and tissue
such softness, such flesh
now ...
so close to being nothing
my etude
not done correctly
breaks the glass, opens
a morning in Pretoria
a morning nervous and yellowish
its guts ripped out
and putrifying
stuffed back into its throat.
The professor and the national party
and Botha
and Oppensheimer the diamond man
were skeptical about
the Bantu in Bothutapswana
goodnight from Pretoria
goodnight from Pretoria

CANTO XIII

I hated evenings like this
when I fall asleep
in the afternoon
and wake up when it has
already turned evening,
a smell of muddy oil
in the air
a scent of dirty water
trapped under the earth,
it would be damp
a breeze every now and again
got through
the grey watery sky,
and they would hang,
the clouds I mean,
there is no one else
in the world
on those evenings
those absolutely quiet evenings
waking up, looking across to the window,
hearing shoes on the pavement outside
hollow heeled, spiked, woman's
and those man's
flat, slap of leather,
slithering,
I know he has a smile
gold teeth in this mouth
perhaps,
rings on his index, middle
and little fingers,
I'm sure he's wearing tan
she, her face is tight
as the pavement and the
heel of her shoe
her mouth is full of sand

her legs are caught
in that hobbled skirt
and the leaves of the trees
above those sounds
of steps
made a deceitful silky sound
like that
there is no one else in the world
on those evenings,
that dog's voice
barking through,
that child screaming
surprised to be awakened,
astonished at the quiet,
so startling,
to wake up at the wrong time,
the man and the woman
knocking at my sleep,
I am afraid of them
I lie still
waiting for them to leave,
the man's smile, his gold
the woman's tight face
her armpits
tight with sand
they hollow and slither
in turn,
cover me like gauze
like a master-weaver spider,
no matter when I am
these unforgiving evenings
fallen asleep and forgotten
centuries in this huge and ruined
room.

CANTO XIV

naked skin woman, run,
legs to silence
bush to water, to snake's
evanescent legs to dark
water, tree unscaled, run
moss to creeping liana,
nothing grows here
nothing except everything
so green it blacks
so green it thinks
of crevices
to moist on, to ponder
things fecund
full breasts of things
naked skin woman, run.
Here I am
rough and green, as it were
brutal as they come
grubby as usual
where is my battle shoe
one boot and a bead
for my navel,
it's all I need,
here my shale skin
battle dress,
green jacket, protect me,
here again
sister dust, comrade water
here I am
ugly and ready,
hand down my juju,
my life stone, sister clay
wet me with some water
dash my breasts over my shoulders

come sister, hold me back
parry enemy!
Naked skin woman dance, run
belly full of wind
I dance, run
my arms then eloquent wisps
worn over this shawl of a face,
something of a poised mantis
so poised, turned to wood
wooden pall for a cracked face
that met itself in the look of
one million coral
naked woman run.
good day sister death,
let us get drunk
let us eat roses
let us eat newspapers,
what will it matter,
here I am
mercifully bare,
prop up my elbows,
my battle points,
throw water on my face,
give me rum,
show me the dog
let me at him,
houngan!
prepare my bier
put sticks and spit,
my back is like iron
there's blood on my forehead
put a cloth to my temples
come sister, hold my cowry

parry enemy!
Naked woman, run
aloneness comes in the end
it covers ground quickly
but to be a bright and violent thing
to tear up that miserable sound
in my ear
I run
my legs can keep going
my belly is wind.

*Winter Epigrams and
Epigrams to Ernesto Cardenal
in Defense of Claudia*
1983

Winter Epigrams

1

A white boy with a dead voice
sings about autumn
who knows what he means!

2

no one notices
the tree in the front yard
of the next apartment building
is dead, again

3

ten months in the cold
waiting
I have forgotten, for what!

4

they think it's pretty,
this falling of leaves.
something is dying!

5

then months in the snow
dashed in this icy gutter
quartered by a Yonge Street wind
snowflakes, brutal as rapists.

6

sick song
for sick leaves
every September, about the first week
a smell of infirmity clasps the air,
it is a warm lake like an old hand
trying to calm a cold city.

7

a coloured boat
sailed on a frozen lake
at Harbourfront
two northern poets, thankfully rescued
by this trip to Toronto, read
about distant grass
about arctic plains
who wants to see, who wants to listen!

8

cold is cold is
cold is cold is
not skiing
or any other foolhardiness in snow.

9

I give you these epigrams, Toronto,
these winter fragments
these stark white papers
because you mothered me
because you held me with a distance that I expected,
here, my mittens,
here, my frozen body,
because you gave me nothing more
and I took nothing less,
I give you winter epigrams
because you are a liar,
there is no other season here.

10

I'm getting old
I know.
my skin doesn't jump any more
I am not young and in the company of people;
I am old and in the company of shadows.
things pass in the corners of my eyes
and I don't catch them,
what more proof do you want, look!
I am writing epigrams.

11

winters should be answered
in curt, no-nonsense phrases
don't encourage them to linger.

12

thank heavens
in the middle of it all
is '1348 St. Clair', 'Hagerman Hall',
Cuty's Hideaway, These Eyes
and El Borinquen,
where you get to dance fast
and someone embraces you.

13

I can wear dirty clothes
under my coat now,
be who I am in my room
on the street.
perhaps there'll be an accident though.

14

I can pile a winter of newspapers
under my desk
cultivate mice which
would be a new twist in this
Vaughan road cockroach belt.

15

it's too cold to go outside,
I hope there won't be a fire.

16

I've found out
staying indoors makes you horny,
perhaps winter is for writing
love poems.

17

snow is raping the landscape
Cote de Neige is screaming
writhing under
winter's heavy body
any poem about Montreal in the winter is pornography.

18

I've never been to the far north/cold,
just went as far as Sudbury,
all that was there was the skull of the earth.
a granite mask so terrible even
the wind passed hurriedly
the skull of the earth I tell you,
stoney, sockets, people
hacked its dry copper flesh.
I've heard of bears and wolves
but that skull was all I saw.
it was all I saw I tell you,
it was enough.

19

I can buy books
which I do not read and cannot afford
and make plans for them to
carry me through my depression,
winter solstice/flesh buckling,
I attempt various standing and sitting positions
until
sadistic February brings me to my knees,
then, I re-examine my life,
in a maudlin fashion,
conclude that I'm worthless
and spend March and April
in a wretched heap
beside the radiator.

20

going in to Sudbury,
brown and white mountains of rock stood up,
a sound like a dull weapon
going against the shield,
once in, you could never come out.

21

I had to leave that town,
that town in the north
where my uncle went for his asthma.
he bought me a guitar,
I had thought before of singing in a café,
I cried to come to Toronto/Yorkville – the Riverboat
where I thought it was hot and open
and my guitar would collect dust.

22

here!
take these epigrams, Toronto,
I stole them from Ernesto Cardenal,
he deserves a better thief
but you deserve these epigrams.

23

the superintendent dug up the plants again,
each June she plants them
each September she digs them up
just as they're blooming,
this business of dying so often
and so soon
is getting to me.

24

someone in the window
across the way
in the brick and red apartment
is drinking coffee,
smoking a cigarette:
the light is on
it is 3 o'clock in the afternoon.

25

In Resolute Bay
they sing better than I

(*Inuit song*)

26

If one more person I meet
In an elevator in July says to me
'Is it hot enough for you?'
or when standing, cold, at a car stop in November,
'How could you leave your lovely sunny country?'
I will claw his face and cut out his tongue.

27

It was not right to say
her face was ruined by alcohol and rooming houses,
it was still there, hanging on to her
cracking itself to let out a heavy tongue
and a voice (if you could call it that).
her eyes opened not out of any real interest, not to see
where she was going, but out of some remembered courtesy,
something tumbled out of her mouth
a Black woman walked by,
one who could not keep a secret,
betrayed the drunken one's counsel,
I'm not crazy, I just want a cup of coffee,
the wounded tongue replied.
I had a subway token and eleven cents
gave her the latter, told her
I knew she wasn't crazy instead of embracing her.
she closed her hand over the coin
and called me 'sucker'.

28

one good day
if I lift the blinds
and the sun through the glass seems warm
and a woman passing wears a windbreaker,
I forgive you everything,
I forget the last hundred harsh white mornings.

29

if it's not out in the morning
then one day is lost,
if it's not seen for weeks
then months are lost,
with long dank spells as this
I pick up the stitches on my funeral shroud.

30

I feel wicked
when there's no snow in December
as if I've willed it so,
I say 'damn good there's no blasted snow';
I have no sympathy for skiers,
I say they enjoy other people's misfortunes,
snow plough drivers and other warm blooded creatures
as for ski resort owners – procurers and panders!
when there's no snow in December
I feel wicked and positively sublime.

31

Montreal is so beautiful
winter is unfortunate.

32

the first goddamn snow!
as usual it caught me
in my fall sweater.

33

Spring?
I wait and wait and wait;
peer at shrubs,
the neighbours don't know what to make
of this crazy Black woman
rooting in their gardens
looking for green leaves;
in only March at that.

34

comrade winter,
if you weren't there
and didn't hate me so much
I probably wouldn't write poems.

35

Bottles of brandy
beer and eggs for breakfast
jogging in 10 degrees below
past the all night donut shop,
marathon scrabble
going to sleep at 5 a.m.
shorten the days before summer.

36

For Filomena Maria

says she turns greenish yellow,
'infesada' in the winter,
far from an Azorian childhood,
cliffs the colour of roses.
language sounding like full kisses in warmer climes
tighten on the lips of this winter:
Saudade Agua Retorta.

37

I've arranged my apartment
so it looks as if I'm not here
I've put up bamboo blinds
I've strung ever green hedera helix
across my kitchen window
I've bought three Mexican blankets
to put on the walls
I've covered the floors in Persian rugs
(or some reasonable facsimile)
hung pictures of Che and my childhood
bought a rattan-chair – peacock throne
and I've papered my book cases with Latin American writers
I feel like I'm in Canton, Oaxaca, Bahrain and Cocale
now,
If only I could get York Borough to
pass a city ordinance authorizing
the planting of Palm trees along
Raglan Avenue –
my deception will be complete.

38

Only the sound of the light poles
only the sound of the refrigerator
only the sound of the stereo
only the sound of the stove
only, all the sounds seem to be connected by electric wires.

39

that a moon has to shine!
that a moon has to battle fascist street lights!
that a moon has to get mixed up
in that sordid business of car lights!
that a moon has to constantly watch for ingénue skyscrapers!
Enough to make a moon undignified.

40

Reading the Corporate Pages

I was thinking
that it was a waste to have a moon here,
a moon is not cost efficient.

41

Just to sabotage my epigrams,
the snow fell,
these three days,
softly.
Throwing a silence on the streets
and the telephone wires,
whiffling against the north side of the trees.
Two days ago it began,
falling,
so slowly,
3 a.m., Sunday driving along Bloor Street,
Tony, Filo, Pat, Roberto and I
singing to Oklahoma, to a sailor in Valparaiso
and to Billie Holiday
with no wind to witness, to curse us
and this tender snow.
Walking down Greensides Avenue now,
I think someone sitting in a house this minute
and looking through a window at this silence,
cannot be a fascist,
Everyone is covered by this silence
no one can be thinking of how to oppress anyone else
they will have to think of how silent it is
and how to shovel this quiet snow,
no one can make a telephone call
or press a button
or utter a racist slur in this gentleness
they will be struck by their own weakness
they will recognize this silence,
this sphinx of a snowfall
Just to sabotage my epigrams,
the snow fell,
these three days,
softly.

42

Monday: I am one of one hundred
against the United States
in a demo for Nicaragua
the snow, still falling, softly.

43

Oh yes, there it is
the kind that grows cruelty
there it is
what a wind!
the kind that gives a headache
that makes a Christian,
that sculpts a grim mouth
there it is
the one that blows on reservations
and Jarvis Street.

44

Charles Fowler – 1981

Spadina and Baldwin –
the last time I saw Charles Fowler
the wind stung him as he took the corner
went straight through, cutting
his grey hair and his sallow skin;
he had spilled out of the Paramount
in a chain reaction to the twelve beers
pitched up by his stomach – gagging him,
trying to make it south on Spadina
his coat abandoned him, colluding
with the vicious wind and his fingers too,
escaping, just when he found them

buttons on his coat would disappear
London where he was born
Montreal where he met Rose
Toronto
eighty years of being mast and sail
to this wind.

45

—winter suicide—

shall I do it then,
now, here,
a riddle for Februarys,
shall I,
here, under this Mexican blanket
clutching my dictionary (Vol. II the shorter
Oxford Marl–Z),
Shall I do it before falling asleep
before the summer comes
before seeing the Chicago Art Ensemble again,
maybe if Betty Carter never sang,
or Roscoe Mitchell never touched a saxophone;
losing my life like that though,
mislaying the damn thing,
and right in the middle of winter,
me!
and it gone
flown
shall I chew the berries
which I collected before the freeze.

46

some one in the window
across the way
above the coffee drinker
stood
watching me
then he showed me his penis,
how quickly we've established this intimacy.

47

coffin of a winter!

48

sweet tyrone
don't fuck up my night,
Halifax to Toronto
in the dead of winter,
my hands are numb,
gimme back my gloves.

49

carabid of a winter
it chews my ears
and my toes
it gnaws on the extremities.

50

season of ambiguity
blinding sun, cold air
days imitating night
me, here.

51

I had planned the answer all my life
rehearsed my 'fuck offs'
practiced my knee to the groin
decided to use violence;
now, leaving the train at Montreal,
gone!
all my rebuttals,
all my 'racist pig'
nothing,
dried up!
iron teeth of the escalator
snickering like all of 'them',
my legs stiff as the cold outside,
my eyes seeing everything in blood,
a piece of cloth,
a white mound of flesh atop
like a cow's slaughtered head,
emitting,
'whore, nigger whore'.

52

at first I thought
it was because I had no money
and no job and no friends
and no home and no food
then I realized that it was because of February again.

53

Two things I will not buy
in this city,
mangoes and poinsettia;
exiled,
I must keep a little self respect.

54

comrade winter,
look what you've done,
I have written epigrams to you,
e'en poems,
can it be that ...?
No, no, I am not your lover,
Perhaps ... your enemy.

Epigrams to Ernesto Cardenal
in Defense of Claudia

1

I've handed out leaflets at subway stations
crying death to the murdering policemen,
I'm sure the RCMP has my name, my picture,
my letters and now my poems.
You don't even return my calls!

2

These verses are for you Ernesto,
not for all my lovers
whom I bad mouth in these lines,
poor things, the were smaller than these epigrams,
but a poet's ego needs entire pages.

3

If you were there when I came home
after that poetry reading on Spadina,
if you were there when I needed no talking
after that man told me that he liked my poems
but not my politics (as if they are different),
if you were there instead of that empty fellow
I slept with,
you would have held my head, kept me warm
and asked me for nothing else.

4

that cold boy I slept with
believed stories
about cannibalism,
he woke up every morning
in the 19th century,
he wore a pith helmet
to hide his black face,
he didn't know Martin and he didn't know Malcolm
or Garvey or Dubois or Angela,
he had been trained to be orderly and genteel
in little England,
not to give an opinion either way,
not even if it concerned him.

5

we could never talk, you and I.

6

one year and a half
I wrestled in the trenches
with opportunists, quasi-feminists and their government
friends;
a struggle like that in some places
would be revolutionary, empower a whole people;
here in Toronto
we get a community service
and a congratulatory letter
from the minister of immigration.

7

The other day
when France and England and America and Canada and West Germany
were deciding about south west Africa
I packed my things for Namibia,
the plane ticket would not have been a problem
if I only had a gun.

8

we could never make love, you and I
it always has an edge to it
a touch of disbelief.

9

poorest Claudia,
to the barrio
to bare feet
to a boy's sweaty hand
to lipstick from America
to the Hilton hotel
to the carnivorous neon signs
to the electricity shortage
to the banks
to a vulgar sunset
to the ocean.

10

oh! Why do you laugh?
so you think making cruise missiles
for human beings
is more sophisticated, more astute
than poison tipped arrows.

11

Often Ernesto,
little girls are quite desperate.

12

How do I know that this is love
and not legitimation of capitalist relations of production
in advanced patriarchy?

13

Often Ernesto,
women are quite desperate.
Often in your glance
we wish to be invisible.

14

so we spent hours and hours
learning Marx,
so we picketted embassies and stood
at rallies,
so it's been 13 years agitating
for the liberation of Africa,
so they still think, I should be in charge
of the refreshments.

15

the last time I fell in love
was 1972,
then there was Chile and Mylai,
all the Panthers were killed,
Angela was sent to jail,
the guy who did that in California
was rewarded in Washington,
Andrew Young gave up a martyr's day
for a corporate suit
and a lot of other betrayals.

16

I can't speak
for girls of the bourgeoisie,
But girls like me can't wait
for poems and men's hearts.

17

some Claudias are sold to companies,
some Claudias sell to street corners,
even debasement has its uptown,
even debasement has its hierarchy.

18

poorest Claudia,
to the love of a poet
to the singing of a madrigal
to the dictator's American shoes
to the wall
to the afternoon blossoms
to the escape across unknown borders
to the perfume of a freedom.

19

nights have waited for me also
hot and desperate, but cool
the weakened street lights
half of the coca cola sign blinking
another country
the boy leaning on the pole at the Esso station
– there's a flower's smell
which wraps around my face in the night
pale, a yellow-petalled whorl
stretched like a tongue
a taste for night insects
blind ephemera fly into the sweet murky smell –
there's an older woman waiting too
near a hibiscus shrub
the face, dark and knowing, her gaze
bigger than the weakened street lights
what had I given
the boy leaning on the pole at the Esso station
– nothing Ma –

20

Beauty for now, is a hot meal
or a cold meal or any meal at all.

21

so I'm the only thing you care about?
well what about the incursions into Angola,
what about the cia in Jamaica,
what about El Salvador,
what about the multi-national paramilitaries
in South Africa,
and what do you mean by 'thing' anyway?

22

If you don't mind,
can I just sit here today?
Can I not be amusing please?

23

when I saw the guerrillas march into Harare
tears came to my eyes
when I saw their feet, a few
had shoes and many were bare
when I saw their clothes, almost
none were in uniform
the vanquished were well dressed.

24

Carbines instead of M16s
manure explosives instead of cluster bombs
self criticism instead of orders
baskets full of sulpher instead of washing.

25

That is how we took Algiers and Ho Chi Minh city and Maputo and
Harrare and Managua and Havana
and St. Georges and Luanda and Da Dang and Tet and Guinea
and ...

26

I wanted to be there.

27

Dear Ernesto,
I have terrible problems convincing
people that these are love poems.
Apparently I am not allowed to love
more than a single person at a time.
Can I not love anyone but you?
signed,
'Desperate'.

28

Of these soccer tournaments, Selwyn,
of this strutting,
of this herding in playing fields,
of this head knocking and ritualistic dirty talk,
of these decorative cheerleaders
and mannequined man-hunters,
of these incantations over smelly socks, jock straps and shorts,
why so grim?

29

you're lucky I have a bad memory
or I'd remember that red hot arrow
in my ribs,
that feeling of turning to water,
I'd recollect that stupefied look I carried
on my face for three years,
all the signs, they said,
you're lucky I have such a bad memory
for names, faces
or I'd remember that I loved you
then.

30

Ars Hominis/the manly arts

Since you've left me no descriptions
having used them all to describe me
or someone else I hardly recognize
I have no way of telling you
how long and wonderful your legs were;
since you've covetously hoarded all the words
such as 'slender' and 'sensuous' and 'like a
young gazelle'
I have no way of letting you know
that I loved how you stood and how you walked,
and forgive my indelicacy,
your copulatory symmetry, your pensile beauty;
since you've massacred every intimate phrase
in a bloodletting of paternal epithets
like 'fuck' and 'rape', 'cock' and 'cunt',
I cannot write you this epigram.

31

At least two poets,
one hundred other women that I know, and I,
can't wait to become old and haggard,
then, we won't have to play coquette
or butch –
or sidle up to anything.

32

Have you ever noticed
that when men write love poems
they're always about virgins or whores
or earth mothers?
How feint-hearted.

33

Ars Poetica

Yes, but what else was done
except the writing of calming lines
except sitting in artsy cafes
talking artsy talk.
what else except marrying three wives
beating them, flying into tantrums,
except tonal voices, bellicose sermons,
self-indulgent dulcimer expurgations
about fathers and women
what else was done, except
a disembodied anxiety, anger unable
to find a table to land or a door to slam
what when the chance to speak is only taken
when it is not necessary, past,
what when the chance is lost,
what when only doodlings mark a great stone
visits to the asylum mark a great poet
and freedom is personal
yes what then was done except a poser
worse, a mole has infiltrated poems.

34

Ars Poetica (II)

Cow's hide or drum
don't tell me it makes no difference
to my singing,
I do not think that histories are so plain,
so clumsy and so temporal;
griots take one hundred years
to know what they say
four hundred more to tell it;
I want to write as many poems as Pablo Neruda

to have 'pared my fingers to the quick'
like his,
to duck and run like hell from numbing chants.

– Pablo Neruda in 'Ars Poetica (I)' for *Fin de Mundo*

35

Ars Poetica (III)
'on being told that being Black is being bitter'

give up the bitterness
he told my young friend/poet
give it up and you will be beautiful.
after all these years and after all these words
it is not simply a part of us anymore
it is not something that you can take away
as if we held it for safekeeping,
it is not a treasure, not a sweet,
it is something hot in the hand, a piece of red coal,
it is an electric fence, touched,
we are repulsed, embraced and destroyed,
it is not separate, different,
it is all of us, mixed up in our skins,
welded to our bones
and it cannot be thrown away
not after all these years, after all these words
we don't have a hold on it
it has a hold on us,
to give it up means that someone dies,
you, or my young poet friend
so be careful when you say give up the
bitterness.
let him stand in the light for a moment
let him say his few words, let him breathe
and thank whoever you pray to
that he isn't standing on a dark street
with a brick,
waiting for you.

36

we have not received the info yet
but a state of siege has been declared,
the corporate generals conferred,
the joint chiefs of staff consolidated.
In 1980
there was a coup, un golpe,
a military junta, or 'djunta'
as their propagandists say, took over,
a military regime seized power
in the United States.
Careful, this is not a metaphor.

37

you can't say that there's rationing here
you can't complain about the meat shortage
we have a good democratic system here in Transkei
you can't say there is only so much milk or so much butter
you can't say that there are line-ups
you can't bad-talk food on this Bantustan
you can't put goat-mouth on it just like that.
If you don't have a cow you can't
say there's no butter.

38

For Grenada

In St. Georges
there are hills, I hear,
to make me tired
and there is work, I know,
to make me thinner.

39

And take these too Ernesto
as I give them
once more with gratitude
I wish I was with you,
you let me look at 'Managua in the evening sky',
such a sky, memorious and red,
repels cruelties from the Honduran border.

40

Imitation of Cardenal

If Hitler waits at the corner of the Schmiedtor
and a girl is walking along the Landestrasse with her mother
and Hitler cannot dance
and everything is full of kisses
and Hitler cannot dance
so Hitler goose steps
and a girl dances with her mother and a cadet
and a girl walking now with her mother, with a cadet
is not to blame because Hitler has no rhythm
and a girl dances with her mother and a cadet
a girl bebops
and Hitler goose steps
and Hitler finger snaps a war song
a girl is not to blame.

41

The night smells of rotten fruit
I never noticed before
the cicala's deliberate tune,
something about it frightens me
as always,
as when hallucinating with a fever
I saw the mother of the almond tree

shadow me in my hot bed.
Say say stay, say go say!
The night decays with fruit
Dense with black arrangements.

42

And I am so afraid
of all of them
and this tenderness.

43

Isn't it fitting
that Black porters guard the portals
of museums in Paris,
themselves bagged
by elephant guns,
set, between the other objects d'art.
Isn't it fitting
that in the Georges Pompidou,
a Black porter
guards Picasso's 'Guitar'.
this must be some frenchman's joke,
some couturier's idea of a wild design.

44

They sent me this envelope yesterday
they sent me this envelope the day before
there was another the day before that
today they sent me a thick book on
Canada's relations with Latin America and the Caribbean,
all of this with no provocation;
Roger says civilisation is paper,
I call this institutional slaughter.

45

his name meant ruler, king in Yoruba
or god or something ...
and even though I was an atheist
and a socialist, I went with him,
not holding his name against him,
liking it because it wasn't
george or harold – slave names! I spat –
what a love! This Yoruba name:
Olu Fisoye Ojo Ajolabi!
beautiful for introductions and greetings,
venerable and original,
grandiose and lyrical as mother earth –
Yoruba Land,
a name like adire cloth
a name like asoke weave
Until he said: 'the poor want to be poor,
nothing's holding them back, they're just lazy.'
then as serf of his majestic name and tradition
of beaten gold,
as serfs will, I shouted at him:
colonized lackey!, comprador!, traitor!,
adire cloth turn to shreds!
death of a closet monarchist! (served me right)
beautiful appellation of contradictions!
I could not live with him
even though he would have paid the rent,
and, well, it was never personal anyway.

46

I've said too much already
dare I name the rest
they'll sue me for my epigrams
ah! What the hell:
Jason, Clyde, Kwesi,
Oh no not dear Harold, Jesus Christ,
the United States, Pinochet,
David, D'aubuisson, Botha
Litton, ibm, Seaga, Tom Adams
colonialism, sleezy Ronald, Thatcher,
apartheid, oops! it's not a human
rights issue, James Bay,
Indian affairs, Sweet Eddie,
Sunday nights ...

47

you say you want me to ...
to what?
no I can't tap dance
at the International Women's Day rally.

48

Claudia dreams birthday cakes
and mauve bougainvillea
Claudia dreams high heeled shoes
orchid bouquets, french perfume,
Sel Duncan Dress band,
the Hilton hotel pool, rum and coke,
commercials of the 'free' world
and men civilized by white shirts.

49

yet a woman is always alone,
a case of mistaken identity
dreams are incognito.

50

y toma estos tambien Ernesto
como yo los doy
una vez mas con gratitud
desearia estar contigo
me dejas mirar a 'Managua en el cielo vespertino'
un cielo asi, memorable y rojo,
repele las crueldades de la frontera hondurena.

(trans. by Rodolio Pino)

51

Let's celebrate hungry!
Let's riot.

52

the boys at the seminary college
climbed over the walls
their mouths were open like hippopotamuses
the girls at the girls Presbyterian school
fed the hippopotamuses stone cookies
from their cooking class
mimosa busy bodied through the niches
of the seminary walls
the Poinciana leered red and yellow
above.

53

one kiss
too suspicious.

54

Cardenal, the truth is that
even though you are not a country
or my grandmother
or coconut ice cream
or Marquez' Autumn of the Patriarch
or Sarah Vaughan
or Cuban music
or Brazilian movies
or Kurosawa
or C.L.R.'s *Black Jacobins*
or Angela
or Guayguayare
I love you for the same things.

Chronicles of the Hostile Sun
1984

Night – Mt. Panby Beach – 25 March 1983

Many years from now
this surf, this night
of American war ships in Barbados,
Mt. Panby beach with its reef
and sea urchins,
this night of tension
and utterly huge ocean,
I see Orion like an imperialist
straddle the half sky,
a drizzle of rain,
wondering how it is possible
to be fearful and fearless together,
drink another beer,
this night may make it to a poem,
how
the surf so unevenly even
surprises me,
the foam shooting sideways along the rock,
something red blinking far in the ocean

Rose belongs to the militia,
the militia is out
rutting in the drizzle and sand,
they are comfy at Camp David,
we are wet and always startled
though for once we have guns,
for this the boy upstairs
– look at his face
so serious and tender –
For this the boy upstairs
must put on his boots and his greens,
and wake me up at 4 a.m.
coming home

First night of the alert,
all of us in Managua
and on Morne Rouge Bay
were insomniac,
forgetting bathing suits and rum punches,
anything we ate tasted like dirt,
like dirt again,
and to think, in the afternoon,
the shallow bay held all our talk
and now the evening
and the radio silenced,
in Matagalpa,
on the market hill,
we bawled at the air,
someone must go through something for this,
only this night
afraid of the sea and what's in it
and the reef
with its molluscs and shooting tide,
what a sound!
like a shot part the ear,
the salivary foam on the teeth of the sand,
what a sound!
fresh and frightening,
snatching what's ours again

You cannot swim on Mt. Panby beach
but you can sit
and drink a beer in the evening,
and let your eyes fool you
about the green flash of the descending sun,
this night,
Orion's sword – a satellite,
this bird of night
lifted itself up around the houses on the hill and the fort,
you'd never think
that three hours ago it lay pink

and purpling, hugging the town,
even kissing us,
now, that preying bird of a night
gives comfort to spy planes

Mt. Panby
ditches in the sand,
the spitting surf,
it may not be enough time
to drink a beer
and it's the only thing that this beach is good for
except for looking at St. Georges,
and only the fort and the church

they have classified photographs,
these American warships
secret snapshots of public places,
technologically touched up
soviet obstacle courses,
they want to invade,
they want to fill our mouths
with medium range missiles,
that is our considered opinion
since, Mt. Panby
is only good for drinking beer
and looking at St. Georges,
and not even the fishmarket,
it must be our mouths they want to fill

This night
with its shamed faced helicopters
may make it to a poem,
this contra of a night
spilled criminals and machismo
on our mountains,
eagle insignaed somocistas
bared talons in Matagalpa

we were silent in the car,
all that we had talked about
may be gone
and on the way to Mama's bar that night
we stopped, drawn to a radio
on the dark street,
then the woman holding it said
it's the same news,
they're in Nicaragua,
we looked at each other,
someone said, "those bastards".
The street was empty
with all of us standing there

Many years from now
how could it be,
sandflies eat the skin on Mt. Panby beach,
facing the ocean
a look from here can only be a wound,
look! The street empty,
and the bar on Ballast Ground Road
and the beach and the reef
and this little bit,
this bay that only knows
the solitary feet of children
splashing in it on Sundays,
this night may make it to a poem.

Calibishie – April 1983

Over Pt. Baptiste,
Marie Galante across the way
on the horizon,
the lights look like a city from here,
mountains from Guadeloupe
disappear in the evening
but Marie Galante looks like a city
to me, from here,
one of those North American ones
with concrete
and the water like a wide pavement
except for the surf,
the breakers in the fishing canal,
Calibishie,
volcanic stains,
indiscriminate hills protrude the ocean,
some naked, some avoiding the rocks,
we swam
played a game or two with Yemaya,
sure that we would walk out,
sure that the intractable land
would remain,
wait for us to have our fun.
I cannot tell you the face of Calibishie
I, never good at describing faces,
least of all
those that hurricanes sculpt,
just at the top of one slate black rock,
a tree
tearing its hair out
stood in this attitude,
hard as the rock,
at times it pretended to be a masthead
in the fashion of those ships,
a tree,
the hypothesis, the grace of a suicide.

Carifuna

This ancient Carib sold me a hat
and sent his ancient son with a gift
for me,
our spectacles did not hide our ancient look,
those ships ...
discovered and killed us both
now we shared the trinkets left.
He gave me a woven bracelet and small basket,
I gave him this poem and
what a face he had,
right away he knew me,
how can I tell you
this charm of ours, this familial gesture
as if we spoke last night,
the forest of tree ferns and lichen,
the ancient Carib,
his ancient son,
our ancient look,
the forests wait for some recovery,
a new road, a parody of our ancient wound
draws new escutcheons,
I left them in the mountain road,
and I took them with me.

To Roseau

Roseau, you humid slum
full of Jean Rhys' ghosts
who smile at me as if they are people,
your buildings structure a time
of lattice worked windows
and lace glimpses of the genteel over us,
Roseau, after I left
I recalled how you really sounded,
it was in children that you sounded best,
a gang of girls burst the humid air
jumping rope
so intensely,
made up their own difficult game,
rivaling the adventure of the hot town,
a chorus of boys too,
one morning,
calling and answering a song,
if I could remember those things,
a universe contained in them,
a separate and complete life,
a game, a cry containing only them,
the lattice work now ornamental.

Vieux Fort: St Lucia

Vieux Fort has its mad people
and its old men playing,
I saw two children with their pot bellies
climb the wood rotted dock
and the member of parliament step
across the pigs and garbage,
and Vieux Fort has the most wicked sky,
a sky of purple puffs, orange swatches,
a vulgar sky,
the young man in the water
sings and exposes himself,
Vieux Fort has a vengeful sky,
a sky of massive death and massive life,
how can you look at it and the stench below
at once.

La Souffriere

leaving Rosehall, Troumaca,
coming down the leeward side,
I could feel how close the sky was,
everywhere this persistent sky,
I was sitting there with it
tied around my head,
a wide grey-black band trailing off,
it was getting dark three steps in front of me,
the three children on the steps had gone home,
in the back of the truck I could touch it.

Rosehall is the top,
past the mud dried yards,
Up at the top leaves in the mornings.

leeward, the quietest of bays,
the most optimistic of people,
walking the dark from the cricket pitch,
twenty miles looking forward and back,
little girl, stop
from Chateau Belart to the hill before Kingstown,
her face toward me
against the immovable dark, shining,
between the wind and the sky,
pitch black now, and her face,
I don't know that I know anything,
that little girl was stronger than I,
but Rosehall, Troumaca, I must tell you
is at the top of the world.

on the windward side,
up Relevel,
Freddie Oliviere fondled his gun
and threatened six generations of estate workers,
sitting in his expensive jeep,
he threatened a woman with a pension

of one dollar a week,
"if I catch any of all you
down in my land …"

Your land!
Freddie Oliviere jumped out of his expensive
japanese jeep,
his gun in his pocket,
self righteous imperialism on his face,
"I work my ass off for this land …"
"You! You work!
you thief poor people arrowroot money!"

the Atlantic on the windward side
throws up a foam like a drunkard,
a white foam vomiting a green belly in its wake,
Freddie Oliviere talked as if he expected their familiar fear,
livid and wounded by their new tone, angry for
the warmth of their fawning and obeisance,
confident that the gun he fondled
and his truck, and his vanload of henchmen behind
would silence these eight old upstarts:
"your land!
you work!
you thief poor people arrowroot money!"

*

Union
ink-blue water
around you, gnarl or crusty turtles
in blue
peacock
blood
batons, heads, blood, jail,
huddle there

For Martin Carter

yes more
finally it is all more
what else
i recollect nothing
a thief has gone with handfuls
chunks pulled away
handfuls of fruit, pink fleshed stories
a thief sipping pernod
with his moustache and his gold rings
and giving interviews to international correspondents
and his lies
let them take the damn thing
the Esquibo and more
there is no flour
and in a place with so much swamp
no rice
and everybody has been to prison
and we must write on toilet paper
or eat it or hush
and never, never for Walter
no words for Walter, no forgiveness
every bit of silence is full of Walter.

At a cocktail party

The Caricom ministers of education
opened their meeting with a cocktail party,
exactly what you'd expect,
what with being literate
these dunces grinned,
what a privilege to hold a scotch
and a broad smile,
what a joy
simpering for the dollar bill
from the USAID and Reagan's
Caribbean Basin Initiative,
these blockheads
who knew no more than the route to Miami
had the estate workers for hors d'oeuvres
and licked their bones after dinner
since the flesh was all gone
with the Geest boat to English housewives'
impeccable taste for bananas on which birds
never alighted.
only one, Jackie Creft,
among them said something about literacy, how gauche,
appalled, a pall fell over the party,
briefly,
they nodded attentively at first
lest it seem that they be dullards
someone dropped a line from Shakespeare
and the general patter continued.

On eavesdropping on a delegation of conventioners at Barbados Airport

you law unions and conventions of wellwishers
looking to be delighted at problems
where were you when they assassinated Allende
and when El Mercurio tried to steal the peoples' revolution
and when the Gleaner shot down that timid Jamaican,
Manley
where were you with your thoughtful questions
your clerical rectitude, your pastorals, your parsimony
your stamps of approval, your burning morality.
you only wanted to come here
because of the sun.
so you could be with someone who wasn't your wife.
because your wrist watches are one hour behind
the whole damn Caribbean must wait
because you do not know that Murdoch and Thomson
owning all the newspapers in the world
is a violation of free speech,
we cannot close down the Torchlight.
your great virtues
nourished on third world slaughter
your clean hands gesturing up the price of gold
what of Pretoria?
I know, it was before your time
past your discerning eye
(countless crimes are)
but closing newspapers turn your stomachs,
armed with a one inch paragraph from Reuters and AP
you can tell if there is no democracy 10,000 miles away.

Stay at home and watch your soap operas
about your free society
where you are free to be a consumer
where you are free to walk the street
where you are free to demonstrate

where you are free to see the secret files on you
where newspapers print what they like
even if they are lies you will not know
truth is free to be fiction
counting is not an exact science.

Eurocentric

There are things you do not believe
there are things you cannot believe
(in fairness I do not mean women here except
jean kirkpatrick and the like)
these things
they include such items as
revolutions, when they are made by people of colour
truth, when it is told by your privilege
percussive piano solos, squawking saxophones
rosa parks' life, besse smith's life and any life
which is not your own,
ripe oranges with green skins,
blacks lynched in the American way,
Orange Free State, Bantustans,
people waking up in the morning, in any place where you
do not live,
people anywhere other than where you live wanting
freedom
instead of your charity and coca-cola,
the truth about ITT or AFL-CIO
until it is a blithe exposé in your newspaper,
women, who do not need men
(even male revolutionaries refuse to radicalize their
balls)
housework
massacres more in number than 1 american officer
4 american nuns,
sugar apples, cutlass mangoes, sapodillas,
and an assortment of fruit
which having never rested on your tongue
you name exotic,
chains other than ornamental ones,
war, unless you see burning children;
hibiscus flowers and anthurium lilies
rain, on a beach in the Caribbean.

*

like the tiniest cricket
killed and stained
green bones
between the pages of my book
like the frogs song
chirped and nightly
suddenly and again
I have discovered
how much we are
how many words I need.

Amelia

I know that lying there in that bed
in that room
smelling of wet coconut fibres
and children's urine
bundled up in a mound
under the pin chenille and cold
sweating sheets
you wanted to escape,
run from that room
and children huddling against you
with the rain falling outside
and flies and mud
and a criminal for a son
and the scent of the sewer heightened
by the rain falling.
on those days
she tried to roll herself
into the tiniest of balls on the bed
on those days she did not succeed
except in turning the bed into a ship
and she, the stranded one
in that sea of a room
floating and dipping
into the waves, the swell
of a life anchored.
I think that she would have been better
by the sea
in Guayguayare,
but in the town
hot with the neighbours and want
she withered and swelled
and died and left me

after years of hiding
and finally her feet fearful and nervous
could not step on asphalt
or find a pair of shoes.
swimming in the brutish rain
at once she lost her voice
since all of its words contained her downfall.

she gargled instead the coarse water from her eyes
the incessant nights
the crickets call
and the drooping tree,
breathed, in gasps
what was left in the air
after husband and two generations of children.
lying in a hospital bed
you could not live by then
without the contradictions
of your own aggrieved room
with only me to describe the parking lot outside
and your promise, impossible,
to buy me a bicycle,
when they brought your body home
I smiled a child's smile of conspiracy
and kissed your face.

I am not that strong woman

I am not that strong woman on the mountain
at Castle Bruce
the mountain squarely below her feet
the flesh bursting under her skin
I cannot hold a mountain under my feet,
she dug yams and birthed a cow
I am not the old one
boxes on her head in Roseau
the metred street, she made one hundred turns in it
the pee streaming from her straddled legs
she stood over the gutter,
the hot yellow stream wet her ankles
and the street,
nor the other one on Church Street
skirt tied around her waist
mad
some aged song shared her lips
for many years with a clay pipe.

I am the one with no place to live
I want no husband
I want nothing inside of me
that hates me
these are walls and niches
park benches and iron spikes
I want nothing that enters me
screaming
claiming to be history,
my skin hangs out on a clothes line
drying and eaten by the harsh sun
and the wind threatens to blow my belly
into a balloon
to hold more confusions,
alone is my only rescue
alone is the only thing I chose.

I'll gather my skin like a washerwoman
her hand insisting the wind out,
I will bare my teeth to the sun
let it feel
how it is to be dazzled.

Amelia continued ...

1. I leave everyone on roads
   I linger until I am late
   I mistake bedrooms for places where people sleep
   I scratch letters on mud slides,
   of late I am called a mule
   not for my hard headedness
   but for my abstentious womb.

2. I am in love with an old woman
   who bequeathed me a sentence or two
   "don't grow up and wash any man's pants,
   not even out of kindness"
   this, and a bit of spittle
   wrapped in old newspaper.

3. now
   I forget
   hemmed in by sieges and military occupations
   languages
   I forget the country
   I forget myself and wave and smile
   against the twentieth century.

4. Presently I have a vile disposition
   it does not appreciate great sunsets
   from "the villa" looking over the carenage,
   old fort and point salines
   not even the afternoon sun
   escapes my criticism.

Anti-poetry

1. It must be nice to only write
    to two or three people
    to send yourself a s.a.s.e. in verse
    then it does not concern you
    whether your poems stink
    or whether they're directing traffic

2. It's hell to keep a crowd waiting
    for words to describe their insanity
    (let me tell you).
    those thin cigarette smoking white guys
    who are poets
    only shit their pants in discreet toilets
    they don't feel the crowd eating their faces
    I have to hustle poems between the dancers and the
    drummers
    insanity has to be put to dance music.

3. It's not that I'm telling you what to do darling
   but get out of it
   it's a nasty business
   you can't make a living
   and your kind don't know nobody in politics
   and besides that ... well let's not continue.

4. If I tell you
   what most concerns me
   You would think my poems not high enough,
   you would forget my metaphors
   and cultivate a scorn for me,
   you would kill the last word
   on your lips about my imagery.

5. It's hell to find pretty words
   to describe shit, let me tell you,
   I may get beaten up and left for dead
   any moment, or more insultingly to the point,
   ignored.

6. If I tell you
   I don't care much for verses
   dropping their patronizing tone
   all over my ghastly life,
   presuming to decorate my dreary interiors,
   taking charge like a general or a mother,
   If I tell you I crave the free life of a hussy;
   the hurtless life of a catholic priest,
   you would drop me like a passenger

7. It's all very well and good
   as an idle pastime
   to stand around on corners
   singing for the hell of it,
   when you ask the pedestrians
   for a grain of rice
   that's when they get nasty my dear,
   and want you to lift up your dress.

8. Some one at a party
   drew me aside to tell me a lie
   about my poems,
   they said "you write well,
   your use of language is remarkable"
   Well if that was true, hell
   would break loose by now,
   colonies and fascist states would fall,
   housework would be banned,
   pregnant women would walk naked in the streets,
   men would stay home at night, cowering.
   whoever it was, this trickster,
   I wish they'd keep their damn lies
   to themselves.

Diary – The Grenada crisis

In the five a.m. dusk
grains of night's black drizzle, first stones
boulders of dark
sprinkle the open face
open eyes, incense of furtive moths
badluck's cricket brown to the ceiling
I am watching two people sleep.

in the morning smoke light
my chest and its arms cover my breasts,
the ground, wet, the night before,
soil scented,
the open vault of the morning,
scented as the beginning and end of everything
after a while, villainy fingers the eyes,
daubs the hills disenchant
and the mouth lies in its roof
like a cold snake.

coals lit
and contained in clay, glowing
a horizon like a morning coal pot,
still an old woman stooping – cold
churches coral their walls on the ridge,
I could exchange this Caribbean
for a good night's sleep
or a street without young men.

the ghost of a thin woman
drifts against the rim of the street,
I thought nothing was passing,
in the grey light before the crying animals,
when I saw her dress and her pointed face,

I am climbing the steps to the garbage dump,
a woman frightens me.

In the pale air overlooking the town
in the anxious dock
where sweat and arms are lost
already,
the ship and the cement
drop against the metal skies,
a yankee paratrooper strangles in this sheet.

prayers for rain,
instead again this wonderful sky;
an evening of the war and those of us looking
with our mouths open
see beauty become appalling,
sunset, breaths of grey clouds streaked red,
we are watching a house burn.

All afternoon and all night,
each night we watch a different
fire burn,
Tuesday, Butler House
Wednesday, Radio Free Grenada
Thursday, The Police Station
A voice at the window looking,
"The whole damn town should burn."
Another, "No too many of us will die."

eyes full of sleep lie awake
we have difficulty eating,
"what's that?" to every new sound
of the war.

In the five a.m. cold light
something is missing,
some part of the body, some

area of the world, an island,
a place to think about,
I am walking on the rocks of
a beach in Barbados
looking to where Grenada was
now, the flight of an American bomber
leaves the mark of a rapist in the room.

of every waking,
what must we do today,
be defiant or lie in the
corridor waiting for them,
fear keeps us awake
and makes us long for sleep.

In my chest,
a green-water well,
it is 5 a.m. and I
have slept with my glasses on
in case we must run.

the last evening,
the dock and the sky make one,
somewhere, it has disappeared,
the hard sky sends
military transports,
the darkness and my shoulders
meet at the neck
no air comes up,
we have breathed the last of it.

In the Grand Etang
mist and damp
the road to Fedon
fern, sturdy,
hesitate
awaiting guerrillas.

October 19th, 1983

this poem cannot find words
this poem repeats itself
Maurice is dead
Jackie is dead
Uni is dead
Vincent is dead
dream is dead
lesser and greater
dream is dead in these Antilles
windward, leeward
Maurice is dead, Jackie is dead
Uni is dead, Vincent is dead
dream is dead
i deny this poem
there isn't a hand large enough
to gesture this tragedy
let alone these words
dead insists itself on us
a glue of blood sticks the rest together
some are dead, the others will not mourn
most wait for the death announcements
Maurice is dead, Jackie is dead
Uni is dead, Vincent is dead
dream is dead
lesser and greater
dream is dead
in these Antilles
windward, leeward
reality will die
i refuse to watch faces
back once again
betrayal again, ships again,
manacles again
some of us sold each other
bracelets, undecorative and unholy,

back to god
i cannot believe the sound
of your voice any longer
blind folded and manacled
stripped

Bernard, Phyllis, Owusu, H.A.
what now
back to jails in these Antilles
back to shackles! back to slavery
dream is dead
lesser and greater
drowned and buried
windward, leeward
a dirge sung for ever
and in flesh
three armoured personnel carriers
how did they feel
shot, shut
across Lucas Street
this fratricide, this hot day
how did they feel
murdering the revolution
skulking back along the road
the people watchful,
the white flare
the shots
the shot, the people running,
jump, flying,
the fort, fleeing
what, rumour, not true
please, rearrested not dead,
Maurice is dead
at 9:30 p.m. the radio
Jackie id dead ...

9:30 p.m. the radio
dream is dead
in these antilles
how do you write tears
it is not enough, too much
our mouths reduced,
informed by grief
windward, leeward
it is only october 19th, 1983
and dream is dead
in these antilles.

October 25th, 1983

The planes are circling,
the American paratroopers dropping,
later Radio Free Grenada stops for the last time
In the end they sang –
"ain't giving up no way,
no i ain't giving up no way"

The OECS riding like birds on a cow
led America to the green hills of St. George's
and waited at Point Salines
while it fed on the young of the land,
eating their flesh with bombs,
breaking their bellies with grenade launchers

america came to restore democracy,
what was restored was faith
in the fact that you cannot fight bombers
battleships, aircraft carriers, helicopter gunships,
surveillance planes, five thousand american soldiers
six Caribbean stooges and the big american war machine,
you cannot fight this with a machete
you cannot fight it with a handful of dirt
you cannot fight it with a hectare of land free from
bosses
you cannot fight it with farmers
you cannot fight it with 30 miles of feeder roads
you cannot fight it with free health care
you cannot fight it with free education
you cannot fight it with women's cooperatives
you cannot fight it with a pound of bananas or a handful of
fish
which belongs to you

certainly you cannot fight it with dignity.
because you must run into the street
you must crawl into a ditch

and you must wait there and watch
your family,
your mother, your sister, your little brother,
your husband, your wife,
you must watch them
because they will become hungry,
and they will give you in to the Americans,
and they will say that you belong to the militia,
or the health brigade,
or the civil service,
or the people's revolutionary army
or the community work brigade,
or the New Jewel Movement –
they will say that you lived in the country,
they will say that you are Cuban,
they will say that you served cakes
at the Point Salines airport fundraising,
they will say that you are human,
they will say
that one day last month
you said that for four and a half years
you have been happy.
they will say all this because they want to eat.

And finally you can only fight it with the silence of your
dead body.

October 26th, 1983

A fortnight like the one in May
without duplicity
sodden and overcast
we would have held them off a few more days,
god, usually so reliable on matters of hardship
could not summon up a drop of rain

October 27th, 1983

And rain does not rust bombers
instead it looks for weaknesses in farm implements

October 27th, 1983 – evening

the sky does not have the decency
to shut up

After ...

1. Those in the market square
   they will betray you
   they will eat your food
   and betray you
   they will lift you on their shoulders
   and they will denounce you
   When push comes to shove
   they will have change for an american dollar
   they will pocket your grief
   they will sing hymns to your killers
   the press will report their happiness

2. when we left
   I took m diary, my passport
   and my Brecht,
   this is security too

3. when we left
   friends watched us go
   "so you're leaving
   how lucky for you"
   and we saw
   their "will you send for me?"

On American numeracy and literacy in the war against Grenada

Counting in american
you start with 600 cubans,
the next figure in that numeracy
is 1100 cubans,
trouble ascending, move to 200 cubans,
Pi equals zero grenadians
which accounts for the resistance in the hills;
when deploying troops
or actually in most cases, thugs,
send 15,000
if 100 dies it's friendly fire
and anyway that's less than if you
only send 500 (percentage wise you know)
when counting casualties in a war
the first is always american,
(for instance the first casualty in El Salvador
as reported in Newsweek was an american
army officer)
the 40,000 salvadoreans are just playing dead
and the grenadians lying face upward in the sun
at Beausejour are only catching flies.

The term "mass grave" does not apply
to those dug by marines or right wing death squads
    in Central America,
A 'pre-emptive strike' or a 'rescue mission'
to those dug by marines or right wing death squads
is not a war,
except to the illiterate and the oppressed
who have no words for death,
therefore no real need for life.

P.S. Amelia

I must write you this, now
after all this time
I was startled that you left
when I think of it,
I am never lonely for anyone
but you

P.P.S. Grenada

I have never missed a place either
except now
there was a house
there was a harbour, some lights
on the water, a hammock
there was a road,
close to the cliffs'
frequent view of the sea
there was a woman
very young
her boy much older,
we planted corn and ochroes
and peas in the front garden
though the rats ate the corn
there was a boat,
I made friends
with its owner and he called
me on his way to work each morning
there was another road, the one to Goave,
all the way up looking back
the rainy season greened the hills
dry spells reddened the flambouyant
there was a river
at Concord
seeing it the first time surprised me
big smooth stones, brown and ashen
and women standing in its water
with washing
there was a farm
on a hillside
as most are, forty acres with a
river deep inside, Jason and Brother-
man picked coconuts, the air,
the brief smell of cloves, Rusty
swam naked in the river's pond
after our descent, Jason's room
reminded me of a house when I was
a child, wooden windows, dated magazines

books and no indoor tap,
there was a wall of rock which sank into the street
in the trees and vine and lizards
it cooled the walk from town,
though town was hot and steep whenever I
got to the market it was worth the task,
there was a spot, in the centre of the women
and the produce, near to the blood pudding vendor
a place where every smell of earth and sweat
assailed the nostrils and the skin, I would
end up coming home, with the scrawniest provisions,
I don't know how, it was those women's eyes
and their hands, I'd pass by the best and
buy from the most poor,
there was a tree
at the head of the beach,
Grand Anse, not in a showy spot
but cool and almost always empty
of tourists
the ocean there was calmer, shallow,
more to Filo's liking
sea grapes, that was what the tree grew
sea grapes, not at all like grapes in North America
a tougher skin, a bigger seed
sweet and sour at once,
there was the carenage, street and harbour
dock and motorway
tied up to it sometimes 'the sea shepherd'
'albatross' 'vietnam' 'alistair'
the boats to Carriacou, banana boat, the 'geest' and
the tourist boat – Cunard, envy and
hatred to these last two
"how many rooms in that boat, you think?"
this from Frederick, he's had to sleep in
one with his mother and her husband
and when they come down from country,
two more children.
there was a street

a few more really, perhaps
twenty or so would be accurate, inclined, terraced,
cobbled or mud
when I first saw them I remember blanching
at the labour and resolve required to climb them
I would give more than imagined to see them
as they were,
there was a night swimming in the dark
Grande Anse, Morne Rouge, La Sagesse, with voices
after and brandy,
there was a woman thin and black like
a stick, though she mistrusted me, a foreigner,
I marveled at her
there was a friend,
named for a greek,
storyteller like his namesake Homer
he would promise a favour this afternoon
and return five days later with a wild tale
about his car, his hands, the priorities
of the revolution and his personal safety
or a fight with his uncle.
the post office, its smell of yellowing paper,
stamps, its red iron mail box, wooden
posts, the custom's house, its stacks
of paper filled out by hand in quadruplicate,
its patience, its frustrated waiting lines
lunch hour, noon to one, everything is shut
the day's heat at its triumph,
there was a path
wet with grass, weedy
stones but people rarely walk there preferring
the high path overlooking the town,
another thing,
on Woolwich road, the view on its left
incline, houses leaning down, lines of clothing
pots and flowering brush, the ever present
harbour framed through bits or wide angled
to Point Salines,

there was an hour actually many when
the electricity broke down,
my sister grew angry and I lit candles
and the lamps
looking forward to their secretness,
even when the electricity returned
and all around put on their fluorescent lights
I left the candles burning.
there was a month when it rained
and I did not have an umbrella
or proper shoes,
more pot holes appeared in the streets
and pumpkin vines grew swiftly over Marlene's
doorstep,
that was when the sand in the ocean shifted
and leveled out the deep shelf,
that was when one day the beach was startlingly empty
that was when the sea became less
trustworthy,
after Dominica, St. Lucia, St. Vincent
I came back with such relief I
talked to the taxidriver from Grenville
all the way home,
Birch Grove, Beaulieu
after Vieux Fort and Marigot this was comfortable.

there was Paul,
he was a farmer and very young,
in St. David he taught those young
still
to take care of the earth,
he prayed for rain and good students,
we went to a cricket game at Queen's Park
I slept through half of it,
it was a Sunday and I shook his hand goodbye
deciding that I was not big enough for him,
Sunday too when we drove up to Mt. Moritz
worried, a group of young men stopped talking
as we passed
then began again "they have no right",
that was in the middle of the crisis
the fallen silk cotton tree lay across the pond
still growing
it was older than all of us put together,
Jomo and Damani showed us their passion
fruit tree and I took photographs of them
on the rise of Mt. Moritz and the sea in back.

there was a little rum and anxiety
about the coming week,
but hope, we did not want the newness
of this place to end
then everyone would lose their memory
as in Macondo
it was a new way of seeing everything
even thought the sky was still oppressive
and the land smelled of hardship
there was a name for all of this, only
it was never said quite well
but had to do with a freeness which the body felt,
a joy even in the heat,
on bad days I went to the sea
after work, I sat with Chris, the bartender
at the Riviera,
I didn't like the proprieters
they only smiled for tourists but Chris
was good company,
he kept my money and an eye on my belongings
while I dove into the water;
just that was enough, so wide, so womanly
the gaze to the horizon,
I would forget to fill my lungs
for hours, looking to this sea,
once I lay down on the edge
afraid to stand
past the cactus and the prickly shrub
at Point Salines' most eastern tip
the sharpened cliff, the dark blue water
the first meeting of the Atlantic and the Caribbean
gave me vertigo,
that was the last time I went there
before the war,
I suppose that now they've strung barbed wire
between the two

there was a mass of insects, beetles
rain flies, nocturnal
moths, ants
they have a nest in the roof
when I think of getting rid of them
the thought that they are of greater number and stronger
holds me back, they liked dead mosquitoes
I pity mosquitoes
they die in atrocious ways
in hot candle wax, in pesticide fumes or
smashed against the walls,
I still have no idea what children talk about
even after eavesdropping on conversations of theirs
I have no memory myself, only
that the subjects were of some importance,
nor of traders
two more months would have been sufficient time
to walk past the crates of fruits and provisions
these women, small and ship-like, broad and shrewd
slowly, listening for their constancy,
there was that night
when Carol took me to the "turtle back"
after the meeting of banana growers
and we talked about how this island
and the others
made us want and sad
that we could neither go nor stay,
looking at my hands, without a mark,
with self-indulgent palms to fondle paper,
I understood my ill-preparedness
for struggle.
when we left
I took my diaries, my passport and my Brecht
this is security too,
"so you're leaving,
how lucky for you, will you send for me?"

Frederick would be alarmed
that I could not be there when the peas came
that some one else would live in the house,
I left that hat, the one the Carib gave to me
the lamp shades, the Mexican blankets, my
dictionaries, my roads, my evenings
that nuisance breadfruit tree, Dominique promised
to cut it before the next flowering ...
of course some little facts,
the sea in the night, that part which
the lights outside the Dome make clear,
is warm
warmer than the air, and the water
becomes something other than water, fog,
it rolls, rather, spreads toward the feet.

Old Pictures of the New World

1. They show tourists rolling
   on beaches in Barbados
   someone told me that this island
   is flat and inescapable
   just right for american military transports,
   this same someone said,
   the topography of the island
   lacking in gradient or thick forest
   gives historical witness to the absence
   of slave rebellions,
   the slaves having nowhere to run
   adopted an oily demeanour.
   How history slaps us in the face,
   using our own hand too.

2. They show an old
   black man
   beckoning racists back
   to the way it was in Jamaica
   a full page ad in the Chicago Sun Times
   the slave catcher, the African one,
   is a little analysed character,
   (being amongst us
   it is embarrassing to admit),
   but in contemporary times
   whenever the IMF raises the price
   on our heads,
   whenever the americans want to buy
   our skins,
   they raise their hands so quickly,
   it shocks us.

3. They show a little grenadian boy
   eating an orange
   with an american soldier
   this is the new picture postcard
   the new commercial for the new right
   the new look for the new colonialism.

4. They show american medical students
   coming back to Grenada
   now it is safe for them to do their praticals
   in imperialism
   and to spit on the population.

5. They show grenadian market vendors
    and taxi drivers
    call Reagan "daddy"
    now we understand the class war
    and patriarchy.

6. They show george shultz
    celebrating the day Columbus discovered Grenada
    he shades his eyes with his hands
    at Queen's Park
    he sees colonies and slaves
    like the celebrity of 1498
    now we know our place.

7. In the end
   I suppose one knows that Eugenia and Adams
   and Seaga are compradors,
   one knows that they are enemies of the people
   and the future,
   one knows these saprophytes
   will eat on colonialism's corpse until it dries
   one knows that they are our class
   enemies
   but one cannot help feeling betrayed by blood,
   one cannot part with the sense of shame
   at their voraciousness and our current defeat.

8. now I am frightened
    to be alone
    not because of strangers,
    not thieves or psychopaths
    but, the state.

9. they think that I'll forget it
    but I won't
    and when they think that I've forgotten
    they will find a note in the rubble
    of the statue of liberty.

For Stuart

a little red neck in Sudbury
(actually a big red neck, more than six feet tall)
invited me to his radio show
whereupon he seized one of my poems
and using it as evidence, called me
a marxist,
(actually the poem was feminist)
I denied it of course, I'm no
dilettante
I can see what's coming in the country,
anyway, he banged his fist and cursed
on the airwaves,
a suspicious red stain appeared
on his big red neck,
and I thought he was going to hit me,
Stuart was with me,
we just got up and walked out
leaving him to compose himself,
but we couldn't understand which of us he meant
(Stuart being jewish and I black)
when he yelled after us to "go back to where
you came from".
When you get called a marxist
(they use it as a curse you know)
for saying that the americans have no damn right
invading Grenada, (besides this calculation being
totally unscientific)
you know what's coming.

*

I'm sick of writing history
I'm sick of scribbling dates
of particular tortures
I'm sick of feeling the boot
of the world on my breast
my stomach is caving in and
I'm sick of hearing chuckles
at my discomfort
I'm sick of doing literacy work
with north Americans
as they choke on their food and
I'm sick of their hunger
I'm sick of writing new names and dates
of endings.

*

I am now in Saskatchewan
on a bus passing through Blackstrap
I doze off watching the snow
interrupted by grain silos
I must explain imperialism again
in a library in Saskatoon
thankfully there are some old CCFers
in the crowd.

*

four hours on a bus across alberta and saskatchewan
not in all the months standing over frozen river
antigonish at the wood stove should not come next to
right wing Calgary which after all is self conscious and
naked oil and people gone apartment for rent only one
woman who gave her room and her boots signal of a heart
and poor amal says that she grows shorter there taking
what is fear to Saskatoon to meet strangers plead innocence
explain why we had guns to defend against nuclear arms
do not remember the trip back edmonton crossed paths with
another third world supplicant before ignorance plead dead
edmonton at the huge warm room warm paths through blind
snow early morning sleeping through fog driving a young
man who likes to wake up early dark in Saskatoon light in
edmonton gin in the union hall in winnipeg you wonder if
anyone sault ste marie lost luggage for three days swapo
visitors will lie in the same bed next night hurried through
library college public hall slide tapes conviction beg for
help to be left alone the sault just over the border american
television canadian will nuke 'em pugnacious boy in one
prairie town proverbial hope fled not seen in him sixties
clarity sits only in the aged here in Toronto the last
solidarity posters insert the newest names of the fallen
can't wait for construction sites to paste their latest position
on angola nicaragua grenada south africa as if people waited
there for pronouncements never struggle but know the correct
position either way taut cafes eager for montreal a woman
at mcgill back of the car from antigonish long road to Sydney
an area of trees hiding the sign to monastery old as 1750
betrayed dropped off in a ship returning cargo of salted cod
nova scotia instead no remembered continent no black star
back in toronto eyes remaining on that area of trees to monastery
but miners in Sydney understand death explosions strikes long
to Sydney bridge cape breton john arthur's humour more familiar
to mirabeau farmers closer than far away toronto he said halifax

two days ago no sign of africville sent to preston by big money
a street in exchange for more of our grief yet above in a church
basement someone thanked us for our concern in our welfare but
america was great plead nothing say thanks leave for cherrybrook
digby truro bus knifing maritime winter short grass
fearing no return from coast comfort here it is possible
to go out jump off the land apologies to new brunswick
newfoundland someone on the phone asking for company
solidarity for loss loved in sauteurs one year do you
know what happened there is everyone alright hoarse voiced
don't know they have people in crates at the airport they
were bombing when you were there grenville too did you
so and so you didn't hear sorrow is the hoarse voice then
the small expectant voice on the other end filling in stories
gaps time between this year and that village between renew
a friend never met before ringing of unfinished in the cold
hotel room 7 a.m. glad to go home only the wind and fog and
weepy Sydney holds the plane to the edge of this continent.

*

the metropolis
blocks of sturdy brick
iron street
concrete tree
planes, helicopters, bombs
will probably never touch this.

*

I am not a refugee,
I have my papers,
I was born in the Caribbean,
practically in the sea,
fifteen degrees above the equator,
I have a canadian passport,
I have lived here all my adult life,
I am stateless anyway.

*

After the glare the red trees the black grass the green sea the bronze sky the black grass the red sky the bronze sea the trees the black trees the red grass the green sea the green sky.

5th anniversary

we drank beer to the revolution
and we imagined mama's bar
and the dancing on the carenage
we savoured what we might
if we were there and if it all
never happened, of course it did
and this fifth must be done in exile
and with an american permit for those at home.

"... Over the radio
I hear the victory bulletings of the scum of the earth ..."

– Brecht – the Darkest Times

The varnished table
beside it, the short wave radio
the foreign news ricochets off the white wall
behind. Spotted at dead mosquito intervals
I listen for what europe is doing. Voice of america is insipid
The BBC tells me when they will attack
disinformation about more killed/under the curfew.
We know that they are coming.

In the small corridor
soft concrete walls absorb the olive paint
minutely cratered and close to the eye's burnt rim
above and pushing the surrounding air away
from the skin. A bomber splits the surface,
the radio – radio free goes silently
wind leaves my centre, to the bottom of the
millennium again.

The old wooden desk,
pamphlet boxes, letter from unions, the minutes
of the central committee of the NJM. Newspaper clippings
I collect any information, photographs, snatches of news
The short wave radio, my fingers coax the dial
adjusting the antennae. I listen for news of uprisings
The americans have given out 20,000 medals
for conquering the hundred and thirty-three square miles
consisting Grenada.

The office outside
against what is an eternity of muted faces
impenetrable city blocks, grey-brown torpor
I have bought my third short wave radio

each hour with priestly reverence it intones
'we're fighting marxist leninist totalitarianism here'
each hour foreign ministers and U.S. congressman
briefed and sheepish on Latin America and the Caribbean
stutter the litany, ... marxist Leninist totalitarianism'.

on the radio a peasant becomes a terrorist
on the radio a bit of land is a grave
on the radio disgusting and brutish again
a message from 1940, national security decision
directive 138, a bill against all acts or likely acts
of international morality,
they're not after criminals,
they're after you.

*

In the hotel
something woke me
there was no noise
no voice
no radio
none of my companions
things would happen now, without me.